Emancipation Proclamation
"Forever Free"

Kevin McGruder, PhD
Velma Maia Thomas

. . . by virtue of the power, and for the purpose aforesaid, I do order and declare that all persons held as slaves within said designated States, and parts of States, are, and henceforward shall be free; and that the Executive government of the United States, including the military and naval authorities thereof, will recognize and maintain the freedom of said persons.[1]

President Abraham Lincoln, January 1, 1863

On January 1, 1863 President Abraham Lincoln signed his name to the Emancipation Proclamation which contained the words at left. He added momentum to a process that had been underway for more than two hundred years—freedom for all people of African descent in the United States.

Emancipation Proclamation: Forever Free honors the 150th Anniversary of the signing of the Emancipation Proclamation. This interactive book explores the events, debates, and shifts in ideas that unfolded in the two centuries before the signing. These changes made the Emancipation Proclamation both necessary and possible.

To the extent that you can, view the events of the past described in this book through the eyes of the participants. They held a wide range of views regarding freedom for people of African descent. Religion, economics, race, social class, and personal experiences influenced their thinking. They were people of the times in which they lived. We may prefer that some of them had arrived at different conclusions on the matter of black freedom, yet attempting to understand why they held their beliefs will provide us with a fuller perspective on the actions that made freedom for African Americans a challenge and ultimately a reality.

On the 100th Anniversary of the Emancipation Proclamation, Martin Luther King, Jr. said that its "... momentous decree came as a great beacon light of hope to millions..." As we celebrate its sesquicentennial, we look back at history afresh, knowing this triumph lights the way for our freedom efforts today.

The Emancipation Proclamation, signed by President Abraham Lincoln, January 1, 1863, declared the enslaved in the Confederate States "forever free." More than 21,000 visitors streamed past this historic document when it was displayed for 36 hours, around the clock from June 20 through 22, 2011 at the Henry Ford Museum in Dearborn, Michigan, as part of the "Discovering the Civil War" exhibition.

At 7 a.m. on June 22, the Emancipation Proclamation was carefully packed and flown back to the National Archives in Washington, DC under tight security.

Contents

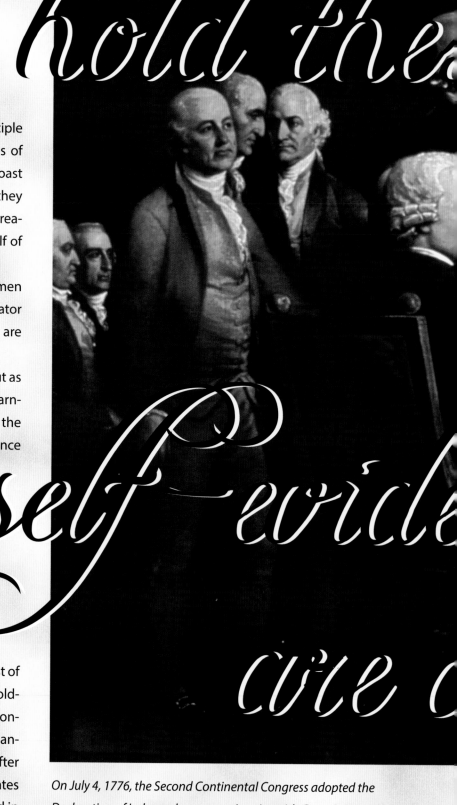

We hold the self-evide cve c

Freedom,

Freedom, or Liberty, was a core principle of the Declaration of Independence. Representatives of Great Britain's thirteen colonies, along the Atlantic Coast of North America, met in Philadelphia in 1776, where they signed the historic document that explained their reasons for separating from the British. Writing on behalf of the Representatives, Thomas Jefferson observed:

We hold these truths to be self-evident, that all men are created equal, that they are endowed by their Creator with certain unalienable Rights, that among these are Life, Liberty and the pursuit of Happiness. [2]

Liberty meant people had the right to move about as they pleased, to own property, and to control their earnings. The term "Liberty" (from Great Britain) became the inspirational word for the American War of Independence (1775–1783). Yet, the signers of the Declaration of Independence did not consider extending to people of African descent the same "unalienable Rights" they described. [3]

Today, we read the words of the Declaration much more inclusively. We almost take for granted that everyone is equal. However, the truth that all people should have the same unalienable rights was beyond the imagination of the Declaration's signers, most of whom were wealthy and many of whom were slaveholders. "Liberty," as we think of it now in our nation, is a concept that has evolved over hundreds of years. The Emancipation Proclamation, signed eighty-seven years after the Declaration of Independence, set the United States on a course that extended the idea of freedom penned in that document to new heights.

On July 4, 1776, the Second Continental Congress adopted the Declaration of Independence, severing ties with Great Britain. Its affirmation that " . . . all men are created equal . . . " is a clarion call that reminds the nation of its founding promise. In this oil canvas, artist

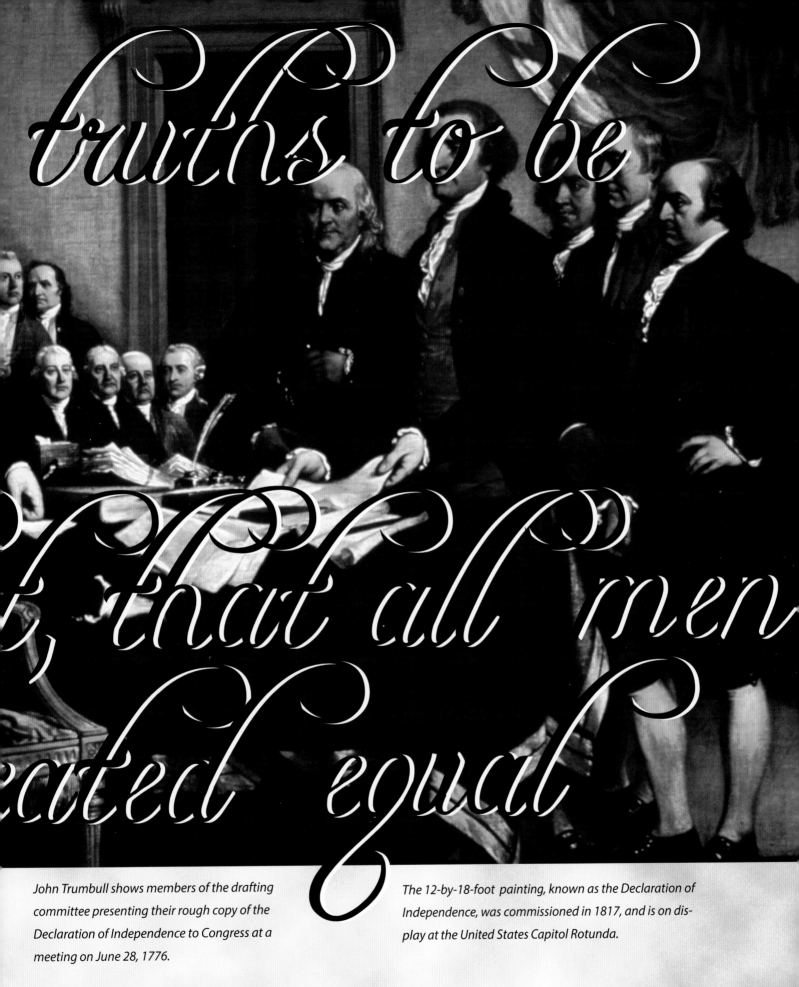

truths to be

that all men

ated equal

John Trumbull shows members of the drafting committee presenting their rough copy of the Declaration of Independence to Congress at a meeting on June 28, 1776.

The 12-by-18-foot painting, known as the Declaration of Independence, was commissioned in 1817, and is on display at the United States Capitol Rotunda.

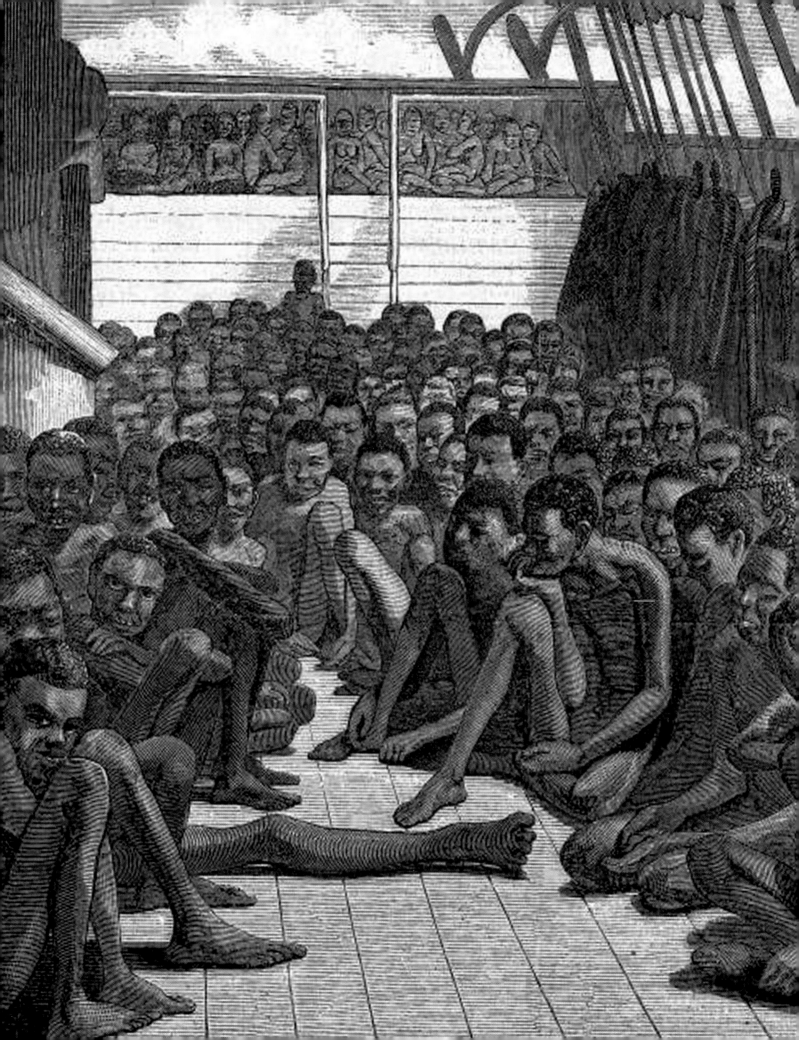

The Constitution was written

during many hot and humid weeks in the summer of 1787, more than a decade following the signing of the Declaration of Independence in 1776. After years of fighting for liberty, the 13 colonies won the War of Independence from Britain, and the Treaty of Paris in 1783 finalized the terms of the end of the War. The United States of America became an independent nation, founded on the idea of liberty.

Before the War was won, the aspiring nation operated under principles contained in the Articles of Confederation. Written in 1777, and ratified/approved in 1781 while the War continued,[4] the Articles acknowledged what the Declaration writers had presumed—all residents of the colonies were not free. Article IV read:

. . . the free inhabitants of each of these States, paupers, vagabonds and fugitives from justice excepted, shall be entitled to all privileges and immunities of free citizens in the several States . . .[5]

As the new nation began to function, some saw the need for a stronger national government than the Articles of Confederation allowed. (The Articles did not, for example, give the national government the ability to raise taxes from the states or permit the calling up of troops from the states.)

A plan to revise the Articles was transformed into a gathering to develop an entirely new document—the Constitution.

During the spring and summer of 1787, delegates of 12 of the 13 states met in Philadelphia at what became known as the Constitutional Convention. (Rhode Island did not send a delegate because it was against a stronger national govern-

Engraving published June 2, 1860, in Harper's Weekly, of the cramped conditions of the more than 600 Africans smuggled on board the bark, Wildfire, which sailed that year from New York, to St. Thomas and on to the Congo, West Africa. The venture was in clear violation of the Act of 1820 which deemed the Trans-Atlantic slave trade piracy—a crime punishable by death. As a bark is a smaller sailing vessel, the crew outfitted it with a deck in the hold, with four feet of clearance, enabling them to house more captives. 450 were on the upper deck, the rest crammed below. According to the reporter, the Africans, were "in a state of entire nudity, in a sitting or squatting posture, the most of them having their knees elevated so as to form a resting place for their heads and arms." The Wildfire was on its way to Cuba, its final destination, when spotted by the U.S. Naval steamer Mohawk. It was captured and towed to Key West, FL, where the captives were held in barracks outside of the city, and later transported to Liberia under an arrangement between the U.S. government and the American Colonization Society. The illegal importation of Africans by U.S. citizens continued almost to the outbreak of the Civil War, despite Congress's attempt to suppress it.

ment.) The delegates debated many issues, such as the structure of government, regulation of commerce, and continuation of slavery.

Some delegates from both the North and South questioned whether the new nation, inspired by the concept of liberty, should continue to condone slavery.[6] The Virginian George Mason declared:

Slavery discourages arts & manufactures. The poor despise labor when performed by slaves. They prevent the immigration of Whites, who really enrich & strengthen a Country. They produce the most pernicious effect on manners. Every master of slaves is born a petty tyrant. They bring the judgment of heaven on a Country.[7]

Gouverneur Morris of Pennsylvania further noted that slavery was a "…nefarious institution… the curse of Heaven on the States where it prevailed."[8]

However, because the delegates' priority at the Constitutional Convention was to strengthen national government, they sought compromises on issues of debate, including slavery.

They agreed to allow the states to count 60 percent of their slave population, along with their free population, to determine the number of Congressional representatives. (**Article I, Section 3, also known as the Three-Fifths Clause.**) The purpose was to establish the number of Congressmen that would represent each state and the amount of taxes each state would pay to the federal government. This gave states with large slave populations more Congressional power than states with the same white populations and few slaves. All free men and women, as well as indentured servants, were fully counted, whether they were qualified to vote or not. Three-fifths (or 60 percent) of all "other persons" were added to that count. The phrase "other persons" was used for the enslaved.

By the 1780s when the Constitution was written, the enslaved population was substantial in southern states and minimal in most northern states. Counting a portion of the slave population to determine Congressional representation meant states with large slave populations received a disproportionate number of Congressmen who advocated legislation in support of slavery.

Rather than outlaw slavery, the delegates at the Constitutional Convention agreed to outlaw the importation of slaves into the United States in 1808, twenty years later. (**Article I, Section 9**) Thus, the continuation of the Trans-Atlantic Slave Trade was protected by the Constitution until 1808.

The business of trading goods for Africans, transporting them across the Atlantic under brutal conditions where many of them died, and selling those who survived as slaves, had supplied the British colonies in North America with labor since 1619. The phrase "importation of such persons" was understood to refer to enslaved Africans.

The Constitutional Convention's delegates also gave slaveholders the right to travel to other states to retrieve their escaped slaves. (**Article IV, Section 3**) This section became known as the Fugitive Slave Clause because it gave slaveholders the right to attempt to re-enslave those persons who escaped and entered other states. Although the word "slave" was never used in the Constitution, these three compromises sanctioned the continued enslavement of people of African descent.[9]

In September of 1787, after eighty-nine days of debate and negotiation, the delegates to the Constitutional Convention signed the final document and returned to their home states to convince the required nine of the thirteen state legislatures to approve the Constitution of the United States of America.[10] The more perfect union, created by the framers of the Constitution, only temporarily tabled the disagreement about the issue of slavery and left to coming generations the task of applying the principles of the Constitution to enslaved people.

At the start of the Civil War in 1861, Charles Francis Adams, Sr., the grandson of John Adams, wrote in his diary, "We the children of the third and fourth generation are doomed to pay the penalties of the compromises made by the first."[11]

We the People

Article I. Section 3 - Representatives and direct taxes shall be apportioned among the several States which may be included within this Union according to their respective numbers, which shall be determined by adding to the whole number of free persons, including those bound to service for a term of years, and excluding Indians not taxed, three fifths of all persons...

Article IV. Section 3 - No person shall be held to service or labor in one State under the laws thereof, escaping into another, shall, in consequence of any law or regulation therein, be discharged from such service or labor, but shall be delivered up on claim of the party to whom such service or labor may be due.

Article I. Section 9 - The migration or importation of such persons as any of the States now existing shall think proper to admit, shall not be prohibited by the Congress prior to the year one thousand eight hundred and eight, but a tax or duty may be imposed on such importation, not exceeding ten dollars for each person.

The Growth of Slavery

is often misunderstood. People of African descent were in the Americas for almost three hundred years by the time the Constitution was written in 1787—and not always as enslaved persons. Africans were among the crews of Christopher Columbus's voyages to the Caribbean from 1492 through 1494. When Spanish explorers arrived in North and South America in the 1500s, people of African descent were among the exploring parties. When the Dutch came to Manhattan in the 1600s, they left behind an African, Juan "Jan" Rodrigues, as punishment.

The status of these Africans ranged from fully free to indentured servants to enslaved. At the time, enslaved did not mean slavery for life. The concept of slavery for life had not yet been established in the Americas.[12]

As the British sought out laborers to cultivate tobacco in Jamestown in 1619, they brought "20 and odd Negroes"[13] to the Virginia colony. It is unknown whether these Africans remained enslaved for life.

By the 1660s, Virginians changed their laws to ensure that enslaved Africans were in bondage for life. Questions arose in the colony if, by virtue of baptism, the enslaved should be set free. In 1667, Virginia's Grand Assembly enacted and declared that baptism did not alter the condition of

Early 1400s Europeans begin to buy African slaves, and the first leg of the slave trade triangle is established.[29]

1502 Juan de Córdoba sends several black slaves from Spain to Hispaniola, the island in the Caribbean that now contains The Dominican Republic and Haiti. In 1517, the first slaves brought directly from Africa arrive to do forced labor on Spanish plantations and mines in the Caribbean.[30]

1526 The history of slave revolts in North America begins with an uprising in the first Spanish settlement in what is now South Carolina.[31]

▲ **1619** In Jamestown, VA, approximately twenty captive Africans are sold into slavery in the British North American colonies.[32]

1623 or 1624 William Tucker is recorded as the first black child born in what would become the United States of America. William is born to Anthony and Isabella who were brought to Jamestown, Virginia in 1619.[33]

bondage. Laying aside this concern, the Assembly nevertheless encouraged slaveholders to offer this sacrament to slaves to propagate Christianity among them. The Virginia laws also changed the status of children born to a free white man and an enslaved woman. Under English law, these children were declared free because their fathers were free. The new Virginia law followed the status of the mother and consequently the children were deemed enslaved.[14]

Africans became enslaved in the Americas and the Caribbean, in part, due to the existence of a form of slavery in Africa long before European contact with the continent began in the 1400s. As prisoners of war, Africans were often enslaved, subsequently becoming household servants, clerks, and mineworkers. However, they were not necessarily slaves for life. Some even married into the families of their African slaveholders. As Europeans came to Africa in the 1400s seeking trading opportunities, African slaves were exchanged as payment for goods purchased by Africans.[15]

Farm workers were increasingly needed with the creation of agricultural colonies in North and South America and the Caribbean. Attempts by Europeans to enslave Native Americans proved unsuccessful; most either escaped capture or died of European diseases. Africans, who had partial immunity to some of these diseases and had better survival rates, were sought as laborers.

During the 1600s and early 1700s, Africans often worked side-by-side with European indentured servants—poor people whose passage to the Americas was paid in exchange for their service, usually for a period of four to seven years. As Europe's economies improved, there was less incentive for poor Europeans to enter into indentured agreements. Soon, enslaved Africans became the primary source of labor in the colonies of the New World. [16]

Efforts to free enslaved Africans began before the founding of the nation and continued as the country grew and expanded. Anti-slavery advocates also sought to prevent the growth of slavery. Publications that condemned African slavery and the slave trade in North America were published as early as 1700. And in 1775, the year before the signing of the Declaration of Independence, the Pennsylvania Society for Promoting the Abolition of Slavery and for the Relief of Free Negroes Unlawfully Held in Bondage was established. [17]

The invention of the cotton gin in 1794 made cotton the most viable cash crop in the South. Although many believed that slavery would eventually no longer be needed, the demand for slave labor to work cot-

1641 Massachusetts is the first colony to legalize slavery.

1650 Connecticut legalizes slavery.

1652 Rhode Island passes laws restricting slavery and forbidding enslavement for more than ten years. [34]

1662 Virginia enacts a law of hereditary slavery, meaning that a child born to an enslaved mother inherits her slave status. [35]

1705 The Virginia Slave Codes, a series of laws regulating interactions between slaves and citizens, consolidates slavery in Virginia and becomes the foundation of its slave legislation. [36]

1740 South Carolina passes the Negro Act, which makes it illegal for slaves to gather in groups, earn money, learn to read, or raise food, and gives slave owners the right to kill rebellious slaves. [37]

▼ **1773 - 1774** Silver Bluff Church of Aiken County, S.C., First African Baptist Church in Savannah, GA, and First Baptist Church of Petersburg, VA are among the earliest black congregations in North America.

ton plantations grew throughout the 1800s. As a result, plantation owners expanded and moved to unsettled areas to establish more cotton farms.

In states such as South Carolina that had large slave populations, almost every aspect of life was influenced by the perceived necessity to maintain a way of life dependent on slave labor. Slave laws were created to define what slaves and slave owners could do. Slave brokers bought and sold slaves at slave markets in most southern cities. White residents volunteered for night patrols to prevent slaves from attempting to escape. Articles appeared regularly advising the best methods for managing slaves.

Although the majority of Southern whites did not own slaves, the slave owning minority held large numbers of enslaved Africans. The wealth they generated through slave labor translated into political power on the local level that allowed them to keep the tax structure low. As a result, southern states did not have public schools and had very few other government services. As with other forms of wealth, slaves were willed to alternate family members upon the death of slave owners, which often led to the separation of enslaved families. Some white southerners were committed to farming without slave labor and maintained small family farms. However, many who did not own slaves hoped to do so one day, since slave ownership was seen as a likely route to wealth. [18]

Even after 1808 when the importation of slaves from Africa was outlawed in the U.S. by the Constitution, the slave trade continued to flourish. Other countries also continued to import African slaves. From 1450-1880, more than ten million Africans were taken from the continent. A substantial number (20 to 50 percent) died on their way to the Caribbean or North and South America during the infamous Middle Passage across the Atlantic. Less than 5 percent of the Africans taken from their homeland made it to North America.[19]

In 1790, at the time of the first U.S. Census, the slave population was 697,624. The greatest number of slaves was imported to the United States in the decade before the 1808 prohibition. This growth in the slave trade, along with birth rates exceeding death rates, led to an enslaved population of 3.9 million by 1860.[20]

Africans in the Caribbean and the Americas created hybrid cultures where they combined their unique

June 1776 Thomas Jefferson drafts the Declaration of Independence.[38]

1785 The New York Manumission Society is created by wealthy, influential, white New York citizens, including such luminaries as John Jay and Alexander Hamilton. They protest the widespread practice of kidnapping black New Yorkers (slave and free) and selling them as slaves elsewhere, and provide legal assistance to both free and enslaved blacks being abused.[39]

1787 The Three-Fifths Compromise is enacted at the Constitutional Convention where the United States Constitution is written.

1787 The Northwest Ordinance is issued. It prohibits slavery, includes a Bill of Rights, and provides for public education.[40]

▼ **1793** The invention of the cotton gin greatly increases the demand for slave labor.

African languages, religions, and culinary traditions with those of the various European cultures of the slaveholders who controlled their lives.[21]

Slave labor became essential to the economies of Southern colonies and an important part of the labor force in some Northern colonies. None of the original thirteen colonies that became states after the signing of the Declaration of Independence outlawed slavery in their new constitutions.

The Constitution protected slavery in the 1800s as the United States expanded its territory, and slaveholders sought to extend slavery to the new territories. In 1803, under the Louisiana Purchase, the U.S. acquired from France more than 800,000 square miles of territory between the Mississippi River and the Rocky Mountains. Settlers consequently moved to the Territory of Missouri in the early 1800s and brought slaves with them. By 1818, when the population had reached 40,000, the Territory applied

for statehood as a slave state, thereby upsetting the current balance of eleven free states and eleven slave states. Northern state members of the U.S. Congress refused Missouri's admittance to the United States as a slave state. [22] When Maine applied for statehood in 1819 as a free state, Southern state members of Congress threatened to prevent its admittance. Facing a possible deadlock, Congress developed the Missouri Compromise of 1820 to allow slavery in the territory below the 36° 30´ latitude line at the base of Missouri and to outlaw slavery in the territory above the line. Missouri was admitted as a slave state, and Maine was admitted as a free state to maintain a balance between slave and free states. [23]

In the 1800s, while southern states were expanding their plantation system, northern states were becoming industrialized. The invention of the steam engine in 1803 revolutionized manufacturing processes. By the 1820s, northern towns began to develop factories, and dependence on slave labor declined. Northern antislavery activities gained force and northern states either abolished slavery outright or enacted gradual emancipation laws to provide freedom at a certain future date. [24] By the 1840s, most northern states had very few slaves, but many continued to maintain strong ties to the slave trade. Since the importation of slaves from outside the United States was prohibited after 1808, shipping cities

1793 The United States passes fugitive slave laws making it illegal to assist slaves who escape to freedom. [41]

1807 Importing of slaves is outlawed by Great Britain and in 1808 by the United States.

1811 Charles Deslondes leads an estimated 500 slaves in an uprising in St. Charles and St. James parishes in the Louisiana Territory. Federal troops suppress the revolt. Deslondes and 20 other slaves are sentenced to death and executed.

▲ **1816** Richard Allen is consecrated as the first Bishop of the African Methodist Episcopal (A.M.E.) Church. African Americans began forming their own churches in the late 1700s.

1820 The Missouri Compromise is enacted when the Missouri Territory's application for statehood is jeopardized over the issue of slavery. [42]

1831 William Lloyd Garrison publishes the first issue of his antislavery newspaper, *The Liberator*. [43]

such as Providence in Rhode Island played important roles in moving slaves within the United States by water. Financial centers such as New York City continued to provide funding for slave purchases, as well as supporting plantation provisions and expansions. Northern textile mills, such as those in Lowell, Massachusetts relied on southern cotton for raw materials. Although slavery had declined in the north, some northerners were still inextricably bound by economics to slavery and the slave trade.

In 1846, the United States went to war with Mexico following a series of territorial disputes. When the Mexican-American War ended with U.S. victory in 1848, the Treaty of Guadalupe Hidalgo gave the United States the territory that is now the U.S. Southwest. Some U.S. slaveholders were already living in the Southwest territory before the war, and their presence increased after the war. By 1850, when California applied for statehood, another negotiation took place resulting in the Compromise of 1850—the series of laws that allowed California to enter as a free state and outlawed the trading of slaves in the District of Columbia. However, the law also strengthened the Fugitive Slave Act, giving penalties to bystanders who refused to assist slave catchers. These slave catchers brought captured individuals to special federal judges, as opposed to local courts, to hear and judge their claims. The escaped slave on trial was not allowed to testify on his or her own behalf. [25]

By the 1850s, the decade preceding the Emancipation Proclamation, the North and South were very different regions. The North had many large cities, industries, networks of railroad lines, diverse and substantial European immigrant labor pools, and relatively literate populations of entrepreneurs and wage earners. In the North were more than 195,000 free African-Americans, who in spite of racial barriers in the areas of education and employment, established businesses, churches and other organizations, and built families. [26]

The South had a few large cities—Richmond, Charleston, and New Orleans—but for the most part it was comprised of smaller towns and rural areas, some of which had plantations of thousands of acres. Slave labor was the foundation of the economy, although the majority of whites, small farmers, had no slaves. The South offered limited opportunities for wage labor and industries. Wealthy landowners and their children were fairly well educated, but the majority of the population—white working farmers and enslaved blacks—was illiterate. [27]

In 1854, when Kansas sought to enter the union, another compromise on slavery was negotiated in Congress. The Kansas-Nebraska Act of 1854 repealed the Missouri Compromise and the 36° 30′ latitude line provisions and replaced it with a system of popular sovereignty, in which whites within the territory voted on

1831 Nat Turner leads a slave rebellion in Southhampton County, VA. [44]

c. 1831 The term "Underground Railroad" is popularly used to name the network helping freed slaves to the North. [45]

1833 The American Anti-Slavery Society promotes the immediate abolition of slavery. [46]

1836 Alexander Lucius Twilight is the first African American elected to public office as a state legislator in the Vermont General Assembly.

1837 New York City hosts the first Convention of the Anti-Slavery Society of American Women, an event attended by both black and white women. [47]

1839 The Amistad Revolt results in one of the most celebrated trials involving the slave trade. Thirty-five Africans of the Mende people win their freedom and are returned to home in Sierra Leone. [48]

1841 Slaves overpower the crew on the Creole, a slave trading ship sailing from Virginia to Louisiana, and successfully sail to the Bahamas where they are granted asylum.

1843 Reverend Henry Highland Garnet's speech, "Let Your Motto Be Resistance," at the National Negro Convention of 1843 in Buffalo, NY, advises the enslaved to refuse to work as a means of resisting slavery. [49]

whether it would be a slave or free territory. Kansas became a literal battleground, as anti-slavery and pro-slavery advocates moved to "Bleeding Kansas" to vote—fighting, and in some cases, killing each other in a bloody conflict. [28]

Undated photograph of the Penn Center School, one of the first for freed slaves. Located on St. Helena Island, S.C., it began in 1862 in the backroom of the Oaks Plantation House as part of the Port Royal Experiment to assist former slaves in transitioning to freedom. Northern white missionaries Laura Towne and Ellen Murray were the first principals. They dedicated forty years to teaching the residents of the Island.

1849 Harriet Tubman escapes from slavery and becomes one of the most effective and celebrated leaders of the Underground Railroad. [50]

1850 The Fugitive Slave Act is passed by Congress and declares that runaway slaves be returned to their masters. [51]

1851 Sojourner Truth addresses the first Ohio Women's Rights Convention in Akron, OH.

1852 Publication of Harriet Beecher Stowe's widely influential *Uncle Tom's Cabin*. [52]

1854 The Kansas-Nebraska Act allows settlers in the territories of Kansas and Nebraska to decide for themselves whether to allow slavery within their borders. It repealed the Missouri Compromise of 1820, which prohibited slavery north of latitude 36°30´. [53]

1859 Abolitionist John Brown attempts an uprising at Harper's Ferry, VA. [54]

1861-1862 Former slaves enjoy freedom on Sea Islands in S.C. in Port Royal Experiment.

1861 The Union Army attacks Fort Sumter, S.C., starting America's four year Civil War. When it is over, slavery as an institution in the United States is abolished. [55]

1862-1865 President Abraham Lincoln pens Preliminary Emancipation Proclamation. Slavery is abolished in the District of Columbia. Congress authorizes president to accept African Americans into military service. The Emancipation Proclamation includes provision enabling African Americans to enter the military (blacks were not allowed in the Civil War army before 1863).

First Louisiana Native Guards are the first African American regiment to be officially mustered into the Union Army. Approximately 200,000 blacks, most of them newly freed or self-emancipated, fight in the Union forces; more than 20,000 are killed in combat.

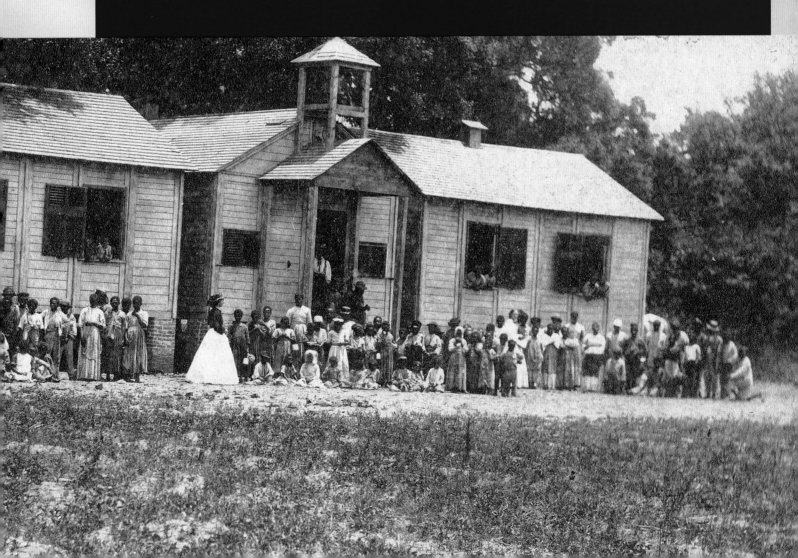

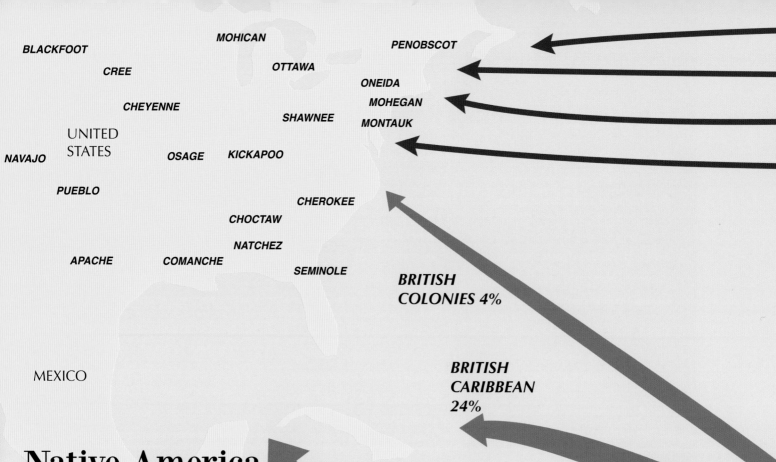

BLACKFOOT
MOHICAN
PENOBSCOT
CREE
OTTAWA
ONEIDA
CHEYENNE
MOHEGAN
SHAWNEE
MONTAUK
UNITED
STATES
NAVAJO
OSAGE
KICKAPOO
PUEBLO
CHEROKEE
CHOCTAW
NATCHEZ
APACHE
COMANCHE
SEMINOLE

BRITISH COLONIES 4%

BRITISH CARIBBEAN 24%

MEXICO

SPANISH COLONIES 13%

FRENCH CARIBBEAN 17%

Native America, Slave Commerce Routes, and European Immigration

Just as Europe is comprised of Britain, Germany and other countries, North and South America were home to many nations, each with their own often highly developed culture and language. The same is true of Africa. Locations of Native Americans and Africans on the map are not precise, but are meant show the very real presence of first nations before European immigration and African slave trade.

Native Americans were part of the story of slavery in the U.S., active forces as slavery grew and even after emancipation in 1863. The history of indigenous Americans and African descended Americans unfolded concurrently. Native Americans were conquered and displaced as plantation owners expanded westward, bringing slave labor. The expansion of slavery meant white control of Native American land and often their forced removal. Indian battles still raged while the Civil War–which ultimately won freedom for blacks–was fought.

This map does not show Asia or the Asian presence in the Americas. For much of the 1800s, territories that would become part of the U.S. experienced some Asian presence–from China, Japan, Korea, India or the Philippines. The vast majority of Asian immigrants during the 1800s were laborers, with large-scale influxes in the 1850s as conflicts about slavery escalated to the breaking point of war.

(Helpful information for this map was found in Give Me Liberty! An American History, Volume 1 by Eric Foner)

SOUTH AMERICA

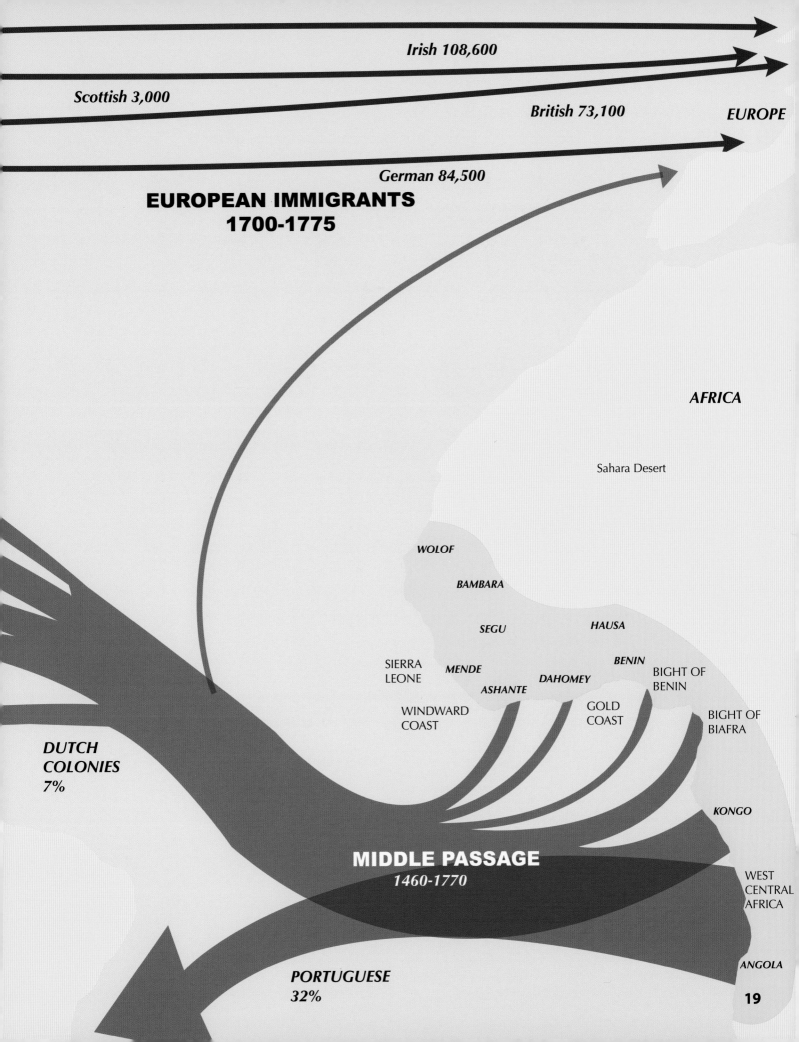

Irish 108,600

Scottish 3,000

British 73,100

EUROPE

German 84,500

EUROPEAN IMMIGRANTS
1700-1775

AFRICA

Sahara Desert

WOLOF

BAMBARA

SEGU

HAUSA

SIERRA
LEONE

MENDE

BENIN

BIGHT OF
BENIN

DAHOMEY

ASHANTE

WINDWARD
COAST

GOLD
COAST

BIGHT OF
BIAFRA

**DUTCH
COLONIES
7%**

KONGO

MIDDLE PASSAGE
1460-1770

WEST
CENTRAL
AFRICA

**PORTUGUESE
32%**

ANGOLA

19

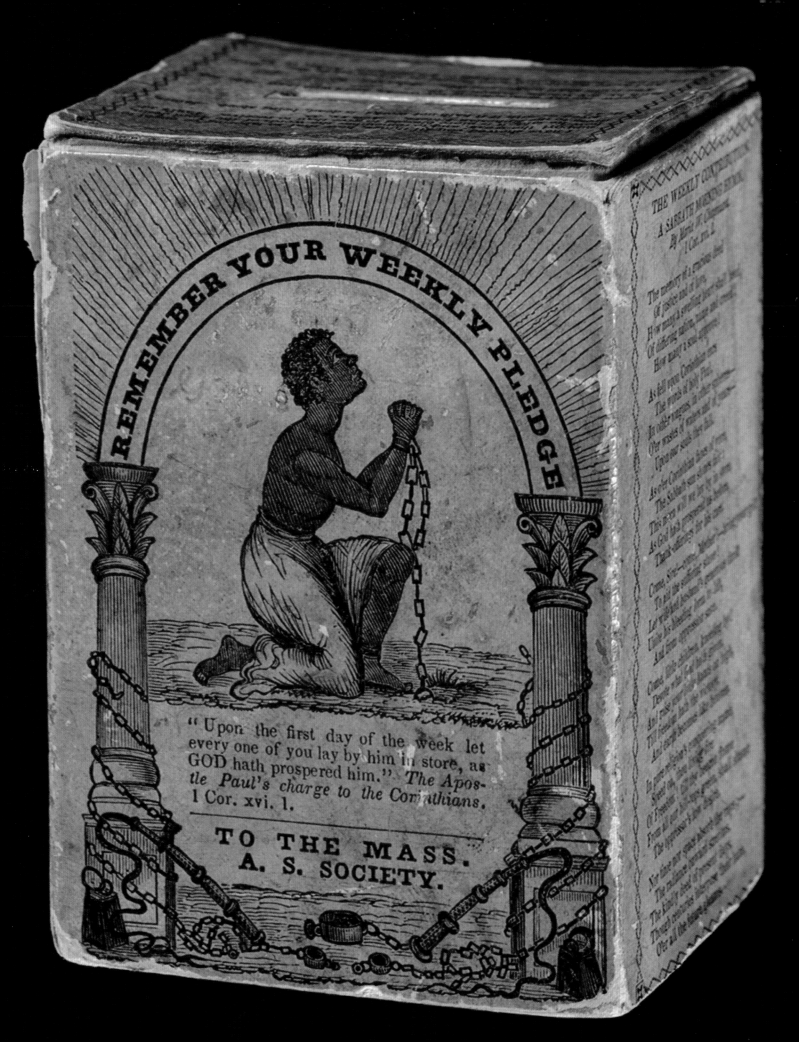

On the Side of Freedom

The Emancipation Proclamation was a victory for those on the side of freedom. Since colonial times, freedom efforts had been varied and numerous. By 1788, when the Constitution was ratified, elite Americans had already formed organizations dedicated to freeing the enslaved. Alexander Hamilton and John Jay, signers of the Constitution, were members of the New York Manumission Society formed in 1785.

Abolitionists helped escaped slaves and fought court battles. Legislators passed laws like The Northwest Ordinance of 1787, governing the settlement of what is now the Midwestern United States, which forbade slavery in the territory. Abolition supporters also formed antislavery societies, as well as organizations to resettle newly freed blacks in West Africa.

Blacks held in bondage rebelled against slaveholders, and free African Americans were active in a wide range of freedom efforts.

Christian Conversion and Manumission

The word manumit means to release from slavery. Individual slave owners sometimes manumitted their slaves or made provisions for slaves to be released upon their deaths. Manumission was a private, legal action taken by individual slaveholders. A religious conversion urged Robert Carter III (1727–1804), a man of vast holdings, to manumit his slaves. In 1777, Carter converted to evangelical Christianity, aligning himself with the Baptists. In 1788, he converted again, this time to the teachings of the Swedish mystic Emanuel Swedenborg. After religious experiences, Carter concluded that slavery was immoral, and in 1791 began a program manumitting 452 slaves on his Nomini Hall Plantation in Westmoreland County, Virginia. That year he filed a "Deed of Gift" with the county. This set in motion a gradual emancipation of his slaves that spanned more than twenty years and continued after his death. Carter chose gradual emancipation to reduce opposition of white neighbors. His is believed to be one of the largest manumissions by a slaveholder in U.S. history.[56]

Manumission Efforts Before the Constitution

Efforts to free the enslaved began early in the nation's history. The Quakers, or the Society of Friends, were among the earliest whites to organize societies and speak against slavery. Although some Quakers owned slaves, members of the religious group later found their faith incompatible with the institution. Quakers, freeborn blacks, former slaves, and others of faith and conscience established or became active in manumission and abolition societies.

1700 Boston Judge Samuel Sewall writes *The Selling of Joseph*, the first antislavery tract published in New England. Sewall condemns African slavery and the slave trade in North America, and cites chapters and verses from the Bible to decry "Man Stealing" as an atrocious crime.

1775 The Pennsylvania Society for Promoting the Abolition of Slavery and for the Relief of Free Negroes Unlawfully Held in Bondage is established. It is the world's first antislavery society and the first Quaker antislavery society. Benjamin Franklin becomes Honorary President of the Society in 1787.

1785 Founding of The New York Society for Promoting the Manumission of Slaves and Protecting Such of Them as Have Been, or may be Liberated. In 1787, the society opened the African Free School, a private institution to educate black children to take their place as equals to white American citizens. African Americans who attended the school included Dr. James McCune Smith, actor Ira Aldridge, abolitionist and minister Henry Highland Garnet, and missionary and educator Alexander Crummell.

Return to Africa

In addition to manumission, some on the side of freedom felt returning freed African Americans to Africa was a compassionate solution to the limitations of everyday movement faced by free blacks due to Fugitive Slave laws. Supporters of colonization believed it was unfair to subject free African Americans to such a harsh atmosphere, where they had little access to education and employment.

They felt free blacks would never be accepted as equals in the United States, that the most humane action was to provide transportation to and assistance in a colony in Africa where they could be free from prejudice and govern themselves. Other whites had no desire to live with African Americans as free men and women. However,

Paul Cuffee

(1759–1817) was a free man born near New Bedford, Massachusetts, to an African father, who was later freed by his Quaker owners and a Native American mother. Cuffee was taught to read by the Quaker family, and at 16, became a sailor on whaling and cargo ships. He rose to Captain, became successful as a merchant businessman owning a fleet of ships, and emerged as one of the wealthiest men of his time in the United States.

A devout Quaker, philanthropist, and abolitionist, Cuffee was troubled by the unfair treatment of blacks, both enslaved and free. In 1813, he sailed to Freetown, a colony in West Africa established in 1787 by Great Britain to resettle freed slaves from London, and later from Nova Scotia and the United States. After assessing the social and economic conditions of the colony, Cuffee met with African leaders there. They convinced him that skilled African Americans would be welcomed. In 1815, after several years of research, Cuffee sailed to Sierra Leone with 38 black colonists, whom he transported at his own expense. In 1817, Cuffee's health began to fail, and he died later that year in the United States, having never returned to Africa.

many African American and some white abolitionists resisted the colonization effort, since America, not the continent of Africa, was their land of birth. The issue was not that men and women of African descent were present in the United States, but that they were denied freedom and equality. At the turn of the nineteenth century, arguments arose for and against transporting free blacks back to Africa, to a colony set up for their benefit.

The American Colonization Society (ACS) was formed in 1816 to transport freeborn or emancipated black men and women to a homeland outside of the United States. The society counted bringing "Christianity and civilization" to Africa and ending the slave trade among its goals.

A major effort to establish a colony for blacks was undertaken by the ACS and Paul Cuffe (Cuffee), a free black ship merchant. In 1815, Cuffee took a group of 38 African Americans to Sierra Leone, an African colony established by the British for newly freed slaves. Two years later, a group of white ACS agents arrived. Initially the settlers struggled to acclimate to the new land. Many died of tropical diseases, and they decided to seek a healthier area north of their original settlement. The location was better, but tensions arose between the African-Americans and the ACS leaders who attempted to exercise leadership over the group.

The ACS did establish a successful settlement that they named "Liberia," drawing on the word liberty. Over the years, other groups of African Americans joined them, and in 1847 African Americans gained control of the colony and declared its independence, becoming the second black republic in the world (after Haiti).

Colonization remained a viable, albeit controversial, option even after the signing of the Emancipation Proclamation. For thousands of freeborn or emancipated African Americans, colonization was the answer to freedom denied on U.S. soil. Between 1816 and 1850, the ACS emerged as the leading voice for relocating free persons of African descent in the United States. In 1819, the Society received $100,000 from Congress for its emigration plan. In January 1820, the ACS's ship Elizabeth sailed from New York to present-day Liberia, West Africa, with three white ACS agents and eighty-eight emigrants aboard.

The venture was difficult, and 22 members of the party died from yellow fever within the first three weeks. The ACS continued its efforts and its recruitment. In 1822, the ACS established a colony that in 1847 became the independent nation of Liberia. From 1825 to 1915 the ACS published the African Repository newspaper, with reports and letters from immigrants. It also established chapters in Maryland, Virginia, and Mississippi.

By 1867, the ACS had assisted moving more than 13,000 African Americans to Liberia.

The Abolitionists

Abolitionists were men and women, black and white, who worked to extol the evils of slavery and end the practice.

From the founding of the nation to the 1830s, those opposing slavery advocated gradual emancipation, limiting the expansion of slavery into new territories, or establishing a colony in Africa for free blacks. The movement took a more urgent stance in 1833, with the founding of the American Anti-Slavery Society (AAS).

Founders William Lloyd Garrison, editor of *The Liberator* newspaper, and Arthur Tappan, businessman and philanthropist, both called for an immediate end to slavery, by questioning the validity of the U.S. Constitution, since it protected slavery.

Abolitionists in the 1830s became increasingly vocal regarding the moral imperative to end slavery. They took full advantage of lower printing costs facilitated by steam printing press technology to spread their message. By 1838, the AAS had 1,350 local chapters and approximately 250,000 members, a huge constituency considering the U.S. at that time consisted of only 26 states, of which thirteen were southern slaveholding states and some northern ones were still in the process of legal abolition or gradual manumission. The nation's population in the 1840 census was roughly 14 million whites and 3 million African Americans, 2.5 million of whom were enslaved. A quarter million members in this radical antislavery organization reflected a groundswell of American sentiment on the side of freedom.

Abolitionists became targets of violent acts by proslavery factions. AAS members were attacked and killed; their printing presses and other property were destroyed.

Members of the AAS disagreed on methods to end slavery. Garrison and Frederick Douglass believed moral suasion was best. Others, like black abolitionist Henry Highland Garnet, advocated political action and rebellion. Despite internal conflict and a division among members, the AAS was key in pushing the issue of slavery to the national political forefront, even to the point of the Civil War.

William Lloyd Garrison (1805–1879) lived by the words he conveyed in the first issue of his newspaper, *The Liberator*: "I am in earnest—I will not equivocate—I will not excuse—I will not retreat a single inch—AND I WILL BE HEARD!" He took an unyielding stance against slavery, appearing to some as immovable, radical, and unrelenting. While many abolitionists favored a gradual end to slavery, Garrison called for immediate emancipation of slaves.

Unlike many, Garrison believed Africans could assimilate into society, that they were entitled the full promise of freedom. He saw the Constitution as inherently flawed because it supported slavery, and sparked controversy by burning a copy of the document. However, for all his fiery rhetoric, he supported nonviolent means to end slavery—a stance he held until the outbreak of the Civil War.

For more than thirty years, Garrison published *The Liberator*. The final issue appeared after the thirteenth amendment to the Constitution was passed in 1865, which ended slavery in the United States. Even in retirement, Garrison continued to write articles, promoting rights of African Americans and women.

Arthur Tappan (1786–1865) was a

cofounder and the first president of the AAS, and one of the leading financial supporters of the antislavery movement.

In 1834, Tappan became the primary target of an outburst of anti-abolitionist rioting in New York. The home of his brother Lewis Tappan, also an abolitionist, was sacked and burned. Arthur Tappan's store was looted as marauders sought to hang him.

In 1835, citizens in East Feliciana, Louisiana, and Mount Meigs, Alabama, offered $50,000 (equivalent to $1,300,000 in 2012 dollars) for Tappan's capture after the AAS mailed 385,000 antislavery pamphlets to the South. [57]

Arthur Tappan resigned from the AAS in 1840, unable to reconcile its radical attacks on the U.S. Constitution and the prominent role of women in the Society. That same year, he and his brother founded the American and Foreign Anti-Slavery Society, and in 1846 organized the American Missionary Association (AMA), which helped to established black colleges after the Civil War.

After the passage of the 1850 Fugitive Slave Act, Tappan became more radical. He declared he was willing to disobey the law for the abolitionist cause. He became a leading financial supporter of the Underground Railroad.

Reverend Theodore S. Wright

(1797–1847). Born to free black parents, Wright was a founding member of the AAS and served on its executive committee until 1840. He led the First Colored Presbyterian Church in New York City and was the first African American to attend Princeton Theological Seminary.

Throughout the 1830s Wright was a spokesperson for the New England Anti-Slavery Society, which sponsored his travels and lectures condemning racial prejudice. Wright's two most influential speeches were "The Progress of the Antislavery Cause" and "Prejudice Against the Colored Man." He wrote several entries and speeches for William Lloyd Garrison's *The Liberator*.

In 1837 at the National Colored Convention

in Buffalo, New York, Wright opposed a resolution advocating black self-defense as "un-Christian." By 1843, however, his views had sufficiently changed; he supported Henry Highland Garnet's call at the National Convention of Colored Citizens in Buffalo for a slave "uprising." A conductor for the Underground Railroad, Wright offered his house at 235 West Broadway as a safe harbor for fugitive slaves.

Abolitionist and Presbyterian minister Henry Highland Garnet

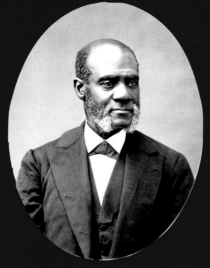

Abolitionist and Presbyterian minister Henry Highland Garnet (1815–1882) stood before the 1843 national Convention of Colored Citizens in Buffalo, New York, and declared that the enslaved in America must "Let Your Motto Be Resistance." His radical speech stunned the crowd and delegates feared this call to rebellion. Garnet's motion was narrowly defeated, losing by only one vote.

A year before that speech, he had stated he believed abolition would come through the political actions of whites. Garnet had also strongly opposed sending blacks to Africa as a solution to the slavery problem, but over time, this view as well began to change, and by 1849 he believed that emigration to Africa could coexist with the fight against slavery at home. Too radical for the Garrisonians, Garnet's influence waned, yet he continued to fight for the rights of African Americans.

In 1865, after the Emancipation Proclamation and end of the Civil War, he became the first black person to deliver a speech to the U.S. House of Representatives.

Garnet died in Liberia, West Africa in 1882, having served as U.S. minister to that country in 1881.

Sojourner Truth

Sojourner Truth (1797–1883) was born Isabella Baumfree and enslaved in Hurley, New York. Having watched three of her children sold away, she escaped to freedom in1826 carrying her infant daughter. After Christian conversion in 1843, she took the name Sojourner Truth, dedicating her life to telling "God's truth."

Traveling to abolition rallies throughout New England, the Midwest, and Middle Atlantic states, Truth became one of the first African-American women who publicly spoke out against slavery and for the rights of women. A compelling orator, she delivered her most famous speech in 1851 asking rhetorically, "Ain't I a woman?" at an Ohio women's rights convention.

At the start of the Civil War, Truth agitated for the inclusion of blacks in the Union Army, and, once they were permitted to join, volunteered by bringing them food and clothes. After emancipation, she continued her fight for African-American and women's rights. Truth died in 1883 at the age of 86. Her obituary in The New York Globe read in part: "Sojourner Truth stands preeminently as the only colored woman who gained a national reputation on the lecture platform in the days before the [Civil] War." [58]

Lydia Maria Child

(1802–1880), popular author of women's books and editor of a children's magazine, began to identify with the antislavery cause in the early 1830s. She said William Lloyd Garrison "got hold of the strings of my conscience and pulled me into reforms." In 1833, in a departure from her earlier works, Child penned **An Appeal in Favor of that Class of Americans Called Africans**. Her

scathing attack on slavery cost her readers and threatened her financial security. Child remained undaunted, taking her seat among abolitionists of her time.

Also a women's rights activist, working with Lucretia Mott and Maria Weston Chapman, she fought for female representation on the board of the AAS. This demand sparked controversy that deeply divided the AAS, which resulted in founding members Lewis and Arthur Tappan resigning in opposition to women serving alongside men. Child, Mott, and Chapman successfully gained seating on the AAS executive board in the 1840s and 1850s, and for three years, Child served as editor of *The National Anti-Slavery Standard*.

Child retained the respect of her male associates. Abolitionist Wendell Phillips stated at her death that she was "ready to die for a principle and starve for an idea. We felt that neither fame, nor gain, nor danger, nor calumny had any weight with her." [59]

Frederick Douglass

Frederick Douglass (1818–1895) emerged as the most influential orator of the abolitionist movement. At age twenty, Douglass escaped from slavery in Maryland to Massachusetts. There, he attended abolitionist meetings and antislavery conventions and subscribed to Garrison's The Liberator. In 1841, Douglass became a lecturer on the Massachusetts Anti-Slavery Convention and joined the AAS. Douglass's speeches were so eloquent that many Northerners found it hard to believe that he had once been enslaved.

Fearing Douglass's former slave owner would come to claim his "property," abolitionists urged Douglass to go to Great Britain, where he could argue for abolition on safer ground. British abolitionists eventually purchased Douglass's freedom, and he returned to the United States.

A prolific writer, Douglass published three autobiographies and edited and published the newspapers *North Star*, *Frederick Douglass' Paper*, and *Douglass Monthly*. He would later differ with Garrison. Douglass advised President Lincoln during the Civil War and recruited black men to serve in the Union Army. After the war, he remained a leading voice, promoting educational, political, and civil rights for African Americans and supporting women's movements. A respected statesman, Douglass noted: "Power concedes nothing without demand. It never has and it never will."

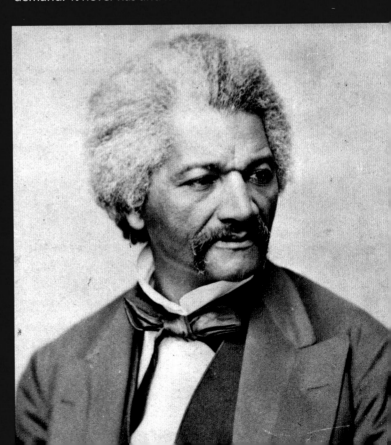

Power of the Pen

Journalists, novelists, and poets led the cultural antislavery crusade. Through the power of the pen and pictures worth a thousand words, they brought the horrors, injustice, and immorality of slavery to the attention of the nation and the world.

White and African-American abolitionist newspapers

Freedom's Journal (1827-1829), editors: Samuel Cornish and John B. Russwurm; the first newspaper in America owned and operated by African Americans.

The Liberator (1831-1866), editor: William Lloyd Garrison

The North Star and Frederick Douglass Paper (1847-1845), editor: Frederick Douglass. Its motto: "Right is of no sex; truth is of no color, God is the Father of us all–and all are brethren"

Anti-Slavery Bugle (1845-1861), New-Lisbon, OH

The National Era (1847-1860), published in Washington, D.C.

Provincial Freeman (1854-1857), Chatham, Ontario, Canada

The Christian Recorder (1852-present), the publication of the African Methodist Episcopal Church. This is the oldest existing black periodical in America and the only newspaper in print that began before the Civil War.

The Pacific Appeal (1862-1870), San Francisco, CA

The Anglo African (1859-1865), New York, New York

Uncle Tom's Cabin was perhaps the most widely read and influential book of the nineteenth century. Harriet Beecher Stowe's novel, inspired by the writing of Josiah Henson, a fugitive slave who escaped to Canada, portrays the evils and immorality of slavery drawing from dozens of scriptural references familiar to readers of that day. Published in 1852, just two years after the 1850 Fugitive Slave Law, *Uncle Tom's Cabin* fueled the crusade to end slavery. The book sold 300,000 copies in the U.S. in one year—second only to the Bible—and one million in Great Britain. By 1857, it had been translated into twenty different languages.

Perhaps the novel's greatest impact was in theaters. It was adapted in many different versions, and played to enthusiastic live audiences throughout the country and world, galvanizing public sympathy for the plight of those in bondage and scorn for their enslavers.

Lore has it that in 1864, President Lincoln greeted Stowe with "So you're the little woman who wrote the book that started this Great War!" Stowe explained her motivation for the book: "I wrote what I did because as a woman, as a mother I was oppressed and broken-hearted, with the sorrows and injustice I saw, because as a Christian I felt the dishonor to Christianity — because as a lover of my country I trembled at the coming day of wrath."[60]

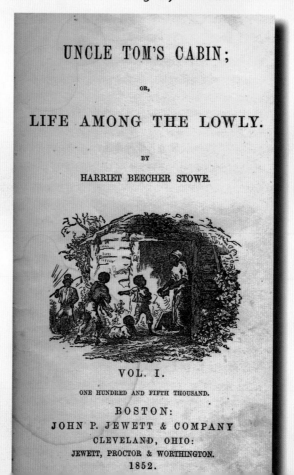

UNCLE TOM'S CABIN;

OR,

LIFE AMONG THE LOWLY.

BY

HARRIET BEECHER STOWE.

VOL. I.

ONE HUNDRED AND FIFTH THOUSAND.

BOSTON:
JOHN P. JEWETT & COMPANY
CLEVELAND, OHIO:
JEWETT, PROCTOR & WORTHINGTON.
1852.

The Bible
Pro-Slavery or the Foundation of Abolitionism?

Equality of races was not a truth that prevailed during the time slavery was practiced in the U.S. Both abolitionists and proponents of slavery claimed biblical support for their positions. Those who believed slavery was wrong—and built the abolitionist movement to a groundswell—often based their actions on belief in God and the Bible. Proponents of slavery claimed it was their God-given right to buy, own and sell slaves and they based their position on the same Bible. Read for yourself key passages from the Bible, in the King James Version, the translation available at that time in history to see how biblical passages were used by both sides.

Genesis 9

18 And the sons of Noah, that went forth of the ark, were Shem, and Ham, and Japheth: and Ham is the father of Canaan. **19** These are the three sons of Noah: and of them was the whole earth overspread.

25 And he said, Cursed be Canaan; a servant of servants shall he be unto his brethren. **26** And he said, Blessed be the Lord God of Shem; and Canaan shall be his servant. **27** God shall enlarge Japheth, and he shall dwell in the tents of Shem; and Canaan shall be his servant.

Exodus 21

1 Now these are the judgments which thou shalt set before them. **2** If thou buy an Hebrew servant, six years he shall serve: and in the seventh he shall go out free for nothing. **3** If he came in by himself, he shall go out by himself: if he were married, then his wife shall go out with him. **4** If his master have given him a wife, and she have born him sons or daughters; the wife and her children shall be her master's, and he shall go out by himself. **5** And if the servant shall plainly say, I love my master, my wife, and my children; I will not go out free: **6** Then his master shall bring him unto the judges; he shall also bring him to the door, or unto the door post; and his master shall bore his ear through with an aul;

At first glance, more verses in the Bible seem to support slavery than speak against it. Some passages, seen here, were even used like an ABCs of slave owning, giving rules and standards for how owners should treat slaves. The problem with using Bible verses to justify slavery is that they must be removed from their original context in order to fit the desired purpose. They have to be taken out of the Bible and read on their own, as done here, without including the surrounding chapters and verses, without understanding the background of the time period and, most important, without reading the entire Bible.

Slavery in biblical

and he shall serve him for ever. **7** And if a man sell his daughter to be a maidservant, she shall not go out as the menservants do. **8** If she please not her master, who hath betrothed her to himself, then shall he let her be redeemed: to sell her unto a strange nation he shall have no power, seeing he hath dealt deceitfully with her. **9** And if he have betrothed her unto his son, he shall deal with her after the manner of daughters. **10** If he take him another wife; her food, her raiment, and her duty of marriage, shall he not diminish. **11** And if he do not these three unto her, then shall she go out free without money.

Leviticus 19

20 And whosoever lieth carnally with a woman, that is a bondmaid, betrothed to an husband, and not at all redeemed, nor freedom given her; she shall be scourged; they shall not be put to death, because she was not free.

Leviticus 25

44 Both thy bondmen, and thy bondmaids, which thou shalt have, shall be of the heathen that are round about you; of them shall ye buy bondmen and bond maids. **45** Moreover of the children of the strangers that do sojourn among you, of them shall ye buy, and of their families that are with you, which they begat in your land: and they shall be your possession. **46** And ye shall take them as an

times was very different from slavery in the U.S. We learn from the Bible that the Hebrew people had a different system of "slavery" from their neighbors. In Hebrew religion and culture, slavery operated more like indentured servitude that allowed people to repay debts through work. Slaves were released every seven years, regardless of whether the debt had been completely repaid, and any remaining amount owed was forgiven. American slavery was not a repayment of a debt, but a lifelong death sentence.

Women, during some eras covered in biblical writing, were seen as property and therefore could be sold as slaves to pay family inheritance for your children after you, to inherit them for a possession; they shall be your bondmen for ever...

Leviticus 27

3 And thy estimation shall be of the male from twenty years old even unto sixty years old, even thy estimation shall be fifty shekels of silver, after the shekel of the sanctuary. **4** And if it be a female, then thy estimation shall be thirty shekels. **5** And if it be from five years old even unto twenty years old, then thy estimation shall be of the male twenty shekels, and for the female ten shekels. **6** And if it be from a month old even unto five years old, then thy estimation shall be of the male five shekels of silver, and for the female thy estimation shall be three shekels of silver.
7 And if it be from sixty years old and above; if it be a male, then thy estimation shall be fifteen shekels, and for the female ten shekels.

Deuteronomy 15

17 Then thou shalt take an aul, and thrust it through his ear unto the door, and he shall be thy servant for ever. And also unto thy maidservant thou shalt do likewise.

Luke 4

14 And Jesus returned in the power of the Spirit into Galilee: and there went out a fame of him through all the region round about. **15** And he taught in their synagogues, being glorified of all. **16** And he came to Nazareth, where he had been brought up: and, as his custom was, he went into the synagogue on the sabbath day, and stood up for to read. **17** And there was delivered unto him the book of the prophet Esaias. And when he had opened the book, he found the place where it was written, **18** The Spirit of the Lord is upon me, because he hath anointed me to preach the gospel to the poor; he hath sent me to heal the brokenhearted, to preach deliverance to the captives, and

debts (Exodus 21:7), but "slavery" in ancient Israel did not allow mothers to be torn from their children. In fact, a man who forcibly slept with a slave woman was required to set her free or marry her (Deuteronomy 21:14), unlike in America, where rape, violence and extraction of children from their mother's breast was in order.

Other types of slavery in the Bible included prisoners placed in bondage to work as repayment for crimes they committed or when conquered people were pressed into service after a war. American slavery never fit any of these molds; rather, it existed as its own warped mutation. Yet, the Bible was used to legitimize harsh behavior toward those in bondage and make victims submit and be subservient toward their masters.

Some Bible commentators who were proponents of slavery, like Finis Dake, took great liberties with

recovering of sight to the blind, to set at liberty them that are bruised...

1 Corinthians 7

21 Art thou called being a servant? care not for it: but if thou mayest be made free, use it rather. **22** For he that is called in the Lord, being a servant, is the Lord's freeman: likewise also he that is called, being free, is Christ's servant. **23** Ye are bought with a price; be not ye the servants of men. **24** Brethren, let every man, wherein he is called, therein abide with God.

Ephesians 6

5 Servants, be obedient to them that are your masters according to the flesh, with fear and trembling, in singleness of your heart, as unto Christ; **6** Not with eyeservice, as menpleasers; but as the servants of Christ, doing the will of God from the heart; **7** With good will doing service, as to the Lord, and not to men: **8** Knowing that whatsoever good thing any man doeth, the same shall he receive of the Lord, whether he be bond or free. **9** And, ye masters, do the same things unto them, forbearing threatening: knowing that your Master also is in heaven; neither is there respect of persons with him.

Colossians 3 and 4

22 Servants, obey in all things your masters according to the flesh; not with eyeservice, as menpleasers; but in singleness of heart, fearing God; **23** And whatsoever ye do, do it heartily, as to the Lord, and not unto men; **24** Knowing that of the Lord ye shall receive the reward of the inheritance: for ye serve the Lord Christ. **25** But he that doeth wrong shall receive for the wrong which he hath done: and there is no respect of persons.
4:1 Masters, give unto your servants that which is just

1 Timothy 6

1 Let as many servants as are under the yoke count their own mas-

particular Bible verses, such as Genesis 9:18-19, and stated that blacks, because they were not white, must be the descendants of Canaan and therefore were supposed to be slaves. Biblical scholars (David M. Goldenberg, for instance) have found no biblical evidence to support this untruth.

Proponents of slavery distorted Scripture. They cherry picked the Bible to fit their ideology. This cherry picking of the Bible by proponents of slavery overlooked specific Bible teaching on the actual wrongs that produced slavery—kidnapping, stealing, torture, murder—and completely negated the actual message of the Bible.

Some of the verses pro-slavery Bible readers ignored are found in the same passages from which they took verses out of context. For example, Exodus 21:1-11 was cited to condone slavery, while Exodus 21:16—an admonition against slavery in the same chapter—was ters worthy of all honour, that the name of God and his doctrine be not blasphemed...

2 And they that have believing masters, let them not despise them, because they are brethren; but rather do them service, because they are faithful and beloved, partakers of the benefit.

Titus 2
9 Exhort servants to be obedient unto their own masters, and to please them well in all things; not answering again; **10** Not purloining, but shewing all good fidelity; that they may adorn the doctrine of God our Saviour in all things.

Philemon
1 Paul, a prisoner of Jesus Christ, and Timothy our brother, unto Philemon our dearly beloved, and fellowlabourer, **2** And to our beloved Apphia, and Archippus our fellowsoldier, and to the church in thy house: **3** Grace to you, and peace, from God our Father and the Lord Jesus Christ. **4** I thank my God, making mention of thee always in my prayers, **5** Hearing of thy love and faith, which thou hast toward the Lord Jesus, and toward all saints; **6** That the communication of thy faith may become effectual by the acknowledging of every good thing which is in you in Christ Jesus. **7** For we have great joy and consolation in thy love, because the bowels of the saints are refreshed by thee, brother. **8** Wherefore, though I might be much bold in Christ to enjoin thee that which is convenient, **9** Yet for love's sake I rather beseech thee, being such an one as Paul the aged, and now also a prisoner of Jesus Christ. **10** I beseech thee for my son Onesimus, whom I have begotten in my bonds: **11** Which in time past was to thee unprofitable, but now profitable to thee and to me: **12** Whom I have sent again: thou therefore receive him, that is, mine own bowels: **13** Whom I would have retained with me, that in thy stead he might have ministered unto me in the

disregarded: "he that stealeth a man, and selleth him . . . . shall surely be put to death." Likewise, the previous chapter of Exodus which contains the Ten Commandments (20:13-15).

Those who used Scripture to justify slavery ignored the foundational message of the Bible. When reading the Bible as a whole, one can only come to the conclusion that the true message of the Bible is love—God's love for all humans and our command to love others.

Despite this overarching message of love and many specific scriptures condemning the practices that together created and upheld the institution of slavery, the Bible was used to rationalize slavery.

Unfortunately, the technique of cherry picking the Bible is still practiced now, 150 years after the Emancipation Proclamation, by those who wish to justify discrimination or hate and to avoid

bonds of the gospel: **14** But without thy mind would I do nothing; that thy benefit should not be as it were of necessity, but willingly. **15** For perhaps he therefore departed for a season, that thou shouldest receive him for ever; **16** Not now as a servant, but above a servant, a brother beloved, specially to me, but how much more unto thee, both in the flesh, and in the Lord? **17** If thou count me therefore a partner, receive him as myself. **18** If he hath wronged thee, or oweth thee ought, put that on mine account; **19** I Paul have written it with mine own hand, I will repay it: albeit I do not say to thee how thou owest unto me even thine own self besides. **20** Yea, brother, let me have joy of thee in the Lord: refresh my bowels in the Lord. **21** Having confidence in thy obedience I wrote unto thee, knowing that thou wilt also do more than I say. **22** But withal prepare me also a lodging: for I trust that through your prayers I shall be given unto you. **23** There salute thee Epaphras, my fellowprisoner in Christ Jesus; **24** Marcus, Aristarchus, Demas, Lucas, my fellow labourers. **25** The grace of our Lord Jesus Christ be with your spirit. Amen.

1 Peter 2
18 Servants, be subject to your masters with all fear; not only to the good and gentle, but also to the froward.

repairing the residual effects of slavery on today's generations.

Believers in the Bible today, mindful of errors made interpreting Scripture during our country's slave era, battle in the abolitionist tradition to dismantle the thinking that isolates individual passages from the whole Bible. The Bible promotes God's love for all humanity and the godly necessity to love each other. It motivates believers to leave behind any tradition that views what is different as less.

To treat anyone in an unloving way is contrary to the true message of the Bible—love.

Natalie Renee Perkins

Negro Spirituals

While proponents of slavery cherry picked passages from the Bible to support their claims, the enslaved embraced the many passages of God's liberation of the oppressed and love for all humanity, including their captors. They created songs of encouragement and deliverance based on Biblical stories and persons. The spiritual "Didn't My Lord Deliver Daniel?" asks that God who delivered Daniel from the lion's den deliver every man—even the enslaved—from the den of bondage.

Abolitionist Frances Ellen Watkins Harper

(1825–1911), a freeborn black woman, was a well-known journalist and poet. A member of the African Methodist Episcopal Church in her youth, she later became Unitarian. Christ was not a distant God to her, but modeled the exalted existence that all human beings could attain. Her *Poems on Miscellaneous Subjects* was published in 1854 with a preface by William Lloyd Garrison. "Bury Me in a Free Land" is among her well-known poems.

Bury Me in a Free Land

Make me a grave where'er you will,
In a lowly plain, or a lofty hill;
Make it among earth's humblest graves,
But not in a land where men are slaves.

I could not rest if around my grave
I heard the steps of a trembling slave;
His shadow above my silent tomb
Would make it a place of fearful gloom.

I could not rest if I heard the tread
Of coffee gang to the shambles led,
And the mother's shriek of wild despair
Rise like a curse on the trembling air.

I could not sleep if I saw the lash
Drinking her blood at each fearful gash,
And I saw her babes torn from her breast,
Like trembling doves from their parent nest.

I'd shudder and start if I heard the bay
Of bloodhounds seizing their human prey,
And I heard the captive plead in vain
As they bound afresh his galling chain.

If I saw young girls from their mother's arms
Bartered and sold for their youthful charms,
My eye would flash with a mournful flame,
My death-paled cheek grow red with shame.

I would sleep, dear friends, where bloated might
Can rob no man of his dearest right;
My rest shall be calm in any grave
Where none can call his brother a slave.

I ask no monument, proud and high,
To arrest the gaze of the passers-by;
All that my yearning spirit craves,
Is bury me not in a land of slaves.

Underground Railroad

The Underground Railroad (UGRR) was a network of safe houses, paths, and secret hideaways along routes from slave states to free territories. It led to freedom within the United States, in Canada, Mexico and to fugitive slave communities in Florida (called "maroons").

Sympathetic blacks and whites risked their lives as "conductors," providing transportation, food, passes, temporary shelter, and clothes to fugitives from slavery. Escapees hid in the false bottoms of wagons, traveled by night, and decoded secret messages along their perilous journey to freedom.

One estimate is that the South lost 100,000 slaves via the Underground Railroad between 1810 and 1850. (The enslaved population in 1810 was 1.2 million and in 1850, there were 3 million African Americans enslaved.)

The impact of the Underground Railroad was greater than the number of escapees. Slave owners convinced Congress to pass the Fugitive Slave Law of 1850, which required that federal marshals arrest alleged runaways or face a $1,000 fine. Persons aiding a runaway also faced a $1,000 fine and up to six months in prison. (At that time, $1,000 was equivalent to nearly $30,000 today.) Nonetheless the enslaved continued to flee, either via the UGRR or individual acts of defiance, and "conductors" white and black aided them.

This detail of the 1893 painting by Charles Webber depicts African Americans in a wagon and on foot, escaping slavery in the freezing cold. It indicates how desperate the enslaved were to risk frigid temperatures with small children for the sake of freedom.

Harriet Tubman

(1830–1913) is the most well-known UGRR conductor, called "the Moses of her people," leading an estimated 300 to freedom. Tubman "never lost a passenger" and eluded slave catchers. During the Civil War, Tubman served as a spy, a military advisor, and a comforter to black Union soldiers. After emancipation and the war's end, Tubman worked on behalf of women's rights and opened a home for the aged. A recent survey named her one of the most famous civilians in American history before the Civil War, third only to Betsy Ross and Paul Revere. She was buried in Fort Hill Cemetery in Auburn, New York, with military honors.

Levi Coffin (1798-1877) was

a devout Quaker, zealous in helping fugitive slaves. He earned the title "President" of the Underground Railroad. In 1826 he and his wife Catherine moved to Newport (now Fountain City), Wayne County, Indiana, where they opened a store. Finding themselves on a route along which escaped slaves passed to free territory, they made their home a safe house. They journeyed at night over secret roads, carrying fugitives to hiding places from which others carried them on to safety.

Coffin purportedly helped more than 3,000 enslaved people escape to freedom in Canada. In 1847, Coffin moved east to

Cincinnati and opened a warehouse that handled goods produced only by free—not slave—labor. [61] During the Civil War, after emancipation, and after the war ended, the Coffins were important figures in the Western Freedmen's Aid Society, which helped educate blacks.

William Still (1821–1902)

rose to become a formidable ally to fugitive slaves crossing into Canada. Still's father was a free man, having purchased his own freedom. His mother tried to escape slavery with their four children, but she was captured. She escaped again, this time taking her daughters, believing her sons would have a better chance of survival under the brutal system. She succeeded and joined her husband. The family later moved to New Jersey where William was born.

At 23, Still moved to Philadelphia and taught himself to read. He later served as secretary to the Pennsylvania Abolition Society and allowed his home to be used on the Underground Railroad. As a "conductor," Still kept detailed records for each person he assisted, including where they came from, how they escaped, and the family they left behind. Still recorded aiding more than 600 individuals in finding refuge in Canada. He assisted one fugitive whom he discovered to be his brother—one of those children his mother had reluctantly left behind.

Still also opened his home to the wife, daughter, and sons of abolitionist John Brown, following his raid on Harpers Ferry. In 1872, Still published his meticulous notes in a book titled *The Underground Railroad*, which remains as one of the most reliable accounts of the activities of the Underground Railroad.

The Secret Road to Freedom

To travel safely to freedom, runaways and the conductors who helped them developed signs, coded messages, and signals to communicate when, where, and how to travel. Directions were hidden in songs, freedom seekers were tucked away in attics and crawl spaces. Men and women wore disguises to outwit authorities. Camouflaged signs helped them find the road to freedom.

The enslaved sang spirituals, songs of deep longing for God's intervention, to end their oppression. The spirituals or "slave songs" sometimes contained hidden meanings, telling when and how to escape. Spirituals were later written and set to musical score. They are still sung in black churches and at Historically Black Colleges and Universities today, in recognition of how God delivered men and women from slavery.

UGRR Coded Messages and Phrases

Agent/Conductor: Operators of the Underground Railroad

Baggage: Fugitive slaves carried by the Underground Railroad worker

Forwarding: Taking escaping slaves from one place to another

Canaan/Heaven: Canada, the free land

Drinking Gourd: The big dipper constellation, which included the North Star. They knew they should always follow the Drinking Gourd because it led the way to the North to freedom

Freedom Train/Gospel Train: The Underground Railroad

The River Jordan: The Mississippi or Ohio River

Load of Potatoes: Fugitive slaves the farmers would hide under the crops in their wagons

"The wind blows from the South today": This told UGRR workers that there were fugitive slaves in the area

"When the sun comes back and the first quail calls" This refers to early spring, which was a good time to escape on the Underground Railroad

"The riverbank makes a mighty good road" this instructed potentially escaping slaves to walk in the river where dogs could not track their scents

"The dead trees will show you the way" a reminder to slaves that, if the North Star was not visible, moss grew only on the north side of dead trees, so they could tell which way to walk

"Left foot, peg foot" footprints left by a wooden-legged UGRR worker as guidelines to the path to freedom

Chariots/traveling shoes phrases often found in spirituals, which refer to preparation to escape and means of travel

Stations the places of safety and temporary refuge where slaves hid along the escape route.

Battle in the Courts

Elizabeth Freeman

(1742 – 1829) was the first enslaved person in the United States to sue successfully for her freedom. At six months old, Freeman (later known as Mombet) and her sister Elizabeth were purchased by John Ashley of Sheffield, Massachusetts. She remained a slave for 40 years.

Freeman sued for her freedom after her mistress, in a fit of anger, swung a shovel at her sister (some accounts say it was Mombet's daughter). Freeman took the blow, never regaining full use of her arm.

She left, never to return; vowing to gain her freedom. She had heard wealthy white men speak of the Bill of Rights and of the 1780 Massachusetts Constitution, which abolished slavery in the state. In 1781, she retained the services of Theodore Sedgewick, a lawyer with antislavery sentiments. Brom, another of Ashley's enslaved, joined the suit.

Sedgewick argued that slavery was inherently illegal under the newly ratified Massachusetts Constitution.

The judge awarded their freedom and ordered Ashley to pay Freeman and Brom 30 shillings and court costs.

Afterward Freeman worked for wages, employed by Sedgewick. She was the first in her family line to agitate for freedom. Her great-grandson, W.E.B. Du Bois (1868–1964), would emerge as a preeminent scholar, editor, and founder of the Niagara Movement, a forerunner to the National Association for the Advancement of Colored People (NAACP). [62]

Dred Scott

Born enslaved in Virginia in 1799, Dred Scott lived in the slave state of Missouri, the free states of Illinois and Wisconsin (territory included in the 1787 Northwest Ordinance), and the slave state of Louisiana, before returning to Missouri with his owner.

In 1846, Scott argued that having lived as a free man in the free states, he could not be returned to enslaved status. He brought suit, Scott v. Sanford, against the state of Missouri and later the federal government, in the hope that the United States Supreme Court would grant him undisputed freedom. In 1857, after ten years of court trials and appeals, and only five years before emancipation, the Supreme Court rendered its decision. The

Court ruled seven to two against Scott, concluding that black people "had no rights in which white men were bound to respect."

Writing in the majority opinion, Chief Justice Roger B. Taney asserted that those of African descent were inherently inferior, and, whether free or enslaved, could never be citizens of the United States. As "non-citizens" they could not sue the federal

government. The opinion ruled that the Northwest Ordinance could not confer freedom or citizenship to nonwhite residents. He also declared that Congress had no authority to prohibit slavery in the territories and ruled the 1820 Missouri Compromise unconstitutional.

Soon after the Supreme Court's ruling, Scott's previous owners, by then opponents of slavery, purchased him and his family and granted them their freedom.

The Court's decision angered abolitionists and further drove the wedge between slaveholding and free states.

It would be Chief Justice Taney who would administer the Oath of Office to President Lincoln on March 4, 1861. [63]

Growing Pressure

Reason, court battles, legislation, and efforts to help escapees were strategies to end slavery. As the nation grew, abolitionists continued these tactics and also began to engage in armed struggle and civil disobedience. This added to the pressure created by acts of violent rebellion committed by those held in bondage. Radical men and women—free and enslaved, white and black—braved death in order to achieve emancipation. Many believed their acts were inspired by God who abhorred slavery (demonstrated by deliverance of the Hebrews from bondage) and who would empower abolitionists with spiritual might. Their actions directly challenged slaveholders, while acts of rebellion by those in bondage made the image of the "happy slave" an outright lie. Freedom would come, if not by the pen, then by the sword.

IIn 1829 David Walker, a free African American living in Boston, published "David Walker's Appeal to the Coloured Citizens of the World," a pamphlet that encouraged the enslaved to rise up against slaveholders. Then in 1831, when Nat Turner's Rebellion resulted in the deaths of at least fifty-five whites in Virginia, slaveholders became increasingly concerned about the unrest of the enslaved.

While the foes of slavery had

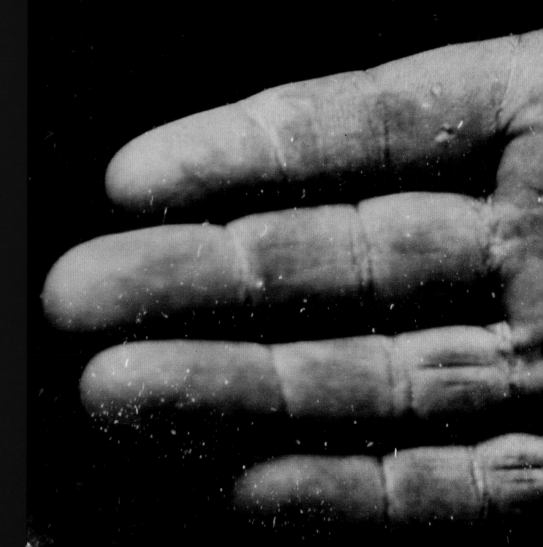

The hand of Captain Jonathan W. Walker, an ardent white abolitionist, bears the brand "S S" for slave stealer. His crime—attempting to free seven enslaved Africans in 1844 by taking them from Florida to the West Indies. Walker fell ill during the voyage, and his crew was unable to continue the journey; however, they were rescued by a "proslavery" ship and taken back to to Florida, and the enslaved were delivered back to their slave holders. Walker was convicted, fined, branded, and placed in solitary confinement for one year. Upon his release, Walker continued with abolitionist fervor, lecturing throughout the country.

for Freedom

been active and vocal for more than a half century—since before the U.S. became a sovereign nation—they became a radical movement in the 1830s, advocating an immediate end to slavery. William Lloyd Garrison formed the American Anti-Slavery Association in1833, and began to publish *The Liberator*, which soon became the leading voice for abolitionism, with Frederick Douglass its most prominent African American member.

At the 1843 National Negro Convention in Buffalo, New York, Rev. Henry Highland Garnet presented a speech "Let Your Motto Be Resistance" advising the enslaved to refuse to work as a means of resisting slavery.

As a result of combined pressure from those on the side of freedom, all the northern states had abolished slavery by the 1840s or instituted "gradual emancipation laws," which provided

---

Poet and abolitionist John Greenleaf Whittier paid tribute to Walker in "The Branded Hand" published in his book Voices of Freedom in 1846. The poem included the passage:
Then lift that manly right-hand, bold ploughman of the wave!
Its branded palm shall prophesy, "SALVATION TO THE SLAVE!"

The photograph of Walker's hand was commissioned by Henry Ingersoll Bowditch (1808–1892), a Boston abolitionist, while Walker was in that city, probably in 1845.

for manumission of the enslaved when they reached a certain age. Black and white abolitionists intensified attention to slavery in the South.

The National Convention of Colored Men, convened in Buffalo in 1843, less than two decades after slavery had been legally abolished in New York State in 1827. Held at the Vine Street AME Church, the purpose of the gathering was to find ways to end slavery.

Organizer and keynote speaker Samuel Davis said fighters in the Revolutionary War had influenced the free men's struggle: "They have taught us a lesson, in their struggle for independence, that should never be forgotten. They have taught the world emphatically that a people united in the cause of liberty are invincible to those who would enslave them, and that heaven will ever frown on the cause of injustice, and ultimately grant success to those who oppose it." [64]

Armed Revolt by the Enslaved

Acts of violent rebellion were planned and committed, successful or not, by the enslaved during the entire era of slaveholding in the U.S. The following are but a few of the most well documented examples.

Gabriel Prosser

Although enslaved, Prosser was allowed to hire out his services as a blacksmith. (The enslaved could occasionally purchase their freedom with such earned money.) Prosser longed for freedom and despised that merchants cheated the enslaved. Inspired by the American Revolution, the uprising in San Dominique 1791, and white artisans who spoke for the working class, Gabriel Prosser developed an elaborate plan to take over the capitol square in Richmond, and take the Virginia governor hostage.

Prosser recruited forces from Richmond, Norfolk, and other Virginia towns. He secured weapons, hammered swords and molded bullets, building an arsenal. August 30, 1800 was the date set for his bold attack.

That evening, a torrential storm arose, washing out roads and bridges, thus forcing Prosser to postpone the attack until the next evening. Two slaves, under pressure, revealed the plan to slaveholders and the uprising never took place. Prosser and those involved in the planned revolt managed to escape, however, they were eventually captured. Prosser stood trial on October 6, 1800, was found guilty, and hanged, along with 26 of his men. Although betrayed by outsiders, those who

stood trial with Prosser remained loyal. A resident of Richmond declared, in a letter dated September 20, 1800, "Of those who have been executed, no one has betrayed his cause. They have uniformly met death with fortitude." [65]

In the aftermath, the American Convention of Abolition Societies issued a public statement affirming that "an amelioration of the present situation of the slaves and the adoption of a system of gradual emancipation… would…be an effectual security against revolt." [66]

Denmark Vesey

Born on the island of St. Thomas, Denmark Vesey arrived in Charleston, South Carolina, in 1783 with his slaveholder. In 1799, Vesey won $1,500 in a lottery and used $600 to purchase his freedom. Law prevented him, however, from purchasing his wife and children. A religious man and a leader, Vesey cofounded an African Methodist Episcopal Church in Charleston, and held small weekly meetings in his home. Membership eventually grew to 3,000. In 1818 authorities interrupted his bible meeting, arrested 140 members and suppressed his church. The church's closure and the continued enslavement of his wife and children fueled Vesey to plan an insurrection to free the enslaved.

In 1822, inspired by the success of the 1791 Haitian revolt, Vesey called together trusted allies and began seriously plotting rebellion where rebels would attack guardhouses and arsenals on June 2, seize arms, kill all whites, burn and destroy the city,

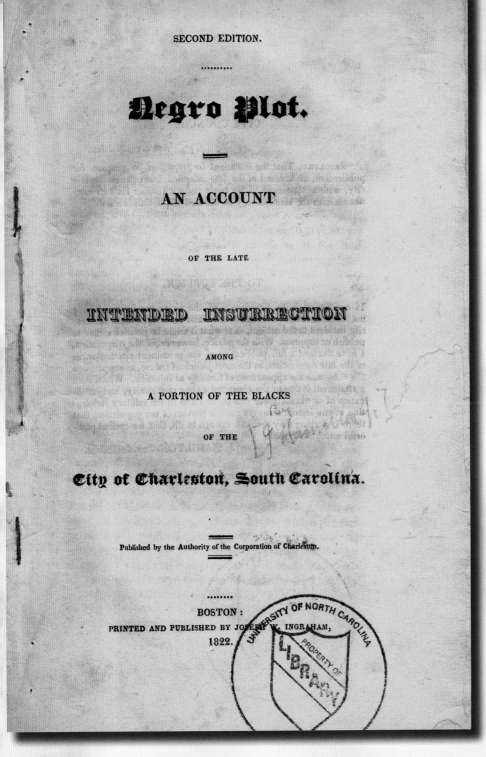

Negro Plot. An Account of the Late Intended Insurrection among a Portion of the Blacks of the City of Charleston, South Carolina. The Negro Plot is a fifty-page book by James Hamilton Jr., who was the intendant (mayor) of Charleston, South Carolina, in 1821, and served as the chief investigator of the Denmark Vesey insurrection. The book gives details of the plan, including brief outlines of Vesey's lieutenants. The text is important because it laid the blame of the insurrection on African-American bad character. He described the enslaved as "having abundant food and excellent clothing" and being misguided by Vesey who was consumed by a "malignant hatred of the whites, and inordinate lust of power and booty."

and free the enslaved. As many as 9,000 free blacks and slaves were rumored to have supported the insurrection. However, a house slave revealed the plot, and Vesey moved the date to June 16. This scheme was also revealed. On the eve of the attack soldiers and patrols were called out en masse, forestalling the rebellion. Vesey and 34 other leaders were captured, tried, and hanged. Although the insurrection failed, Vesey was hailed as a martyr. Years later, the first black regiment of the Civil War called out "Remember Denmark Vesey of Charleston" as its battle cry.

Nat Turner led the bloodiest uprising of the enslaved on United States soil. Born enslaved on October 3, 1800 in South Hampton, Virginia and sold twice, he succeeded where Gabriel Prosser and Denmark Vesey were thwarted.

Turner was revered by the enslaved community as a child with a special calling and mystical gifts because he often spoke of events that took place before his birth. A religious man, Turner had several visions he believed were messages from God to tear down the institution of slavery. In one vision, he saw white spirits and black spirits engaged in armed struggle and heard a voice saying, "Such is your luck, such you are called to see, and let it come rough or smooth, you must surely bare it." He was moved to action by his third vision, of which he would say, "And by signs in the heavens that it would make known to me when I should commence the great work, and until the first sign appeared I should conceal it from the knowledge of men; and on the appearance of the sign... I should

arise and prepare myself and slay my enemies with their own weapons." [67]

A solar eclipse in February 1831 inspired Turner to share his plan to slay slaveholders with his trusted friends. The attack, originally planned for July 4 was pushed to August 13, when Turner was taken ill. That day in August, the sky turned to greenish blue color, and Turner took it as a sign to strike soon. On August 21, Turner and his men retreated to the woods where they fasted and planned. The next morning, they attacked. Their first victims were Turner's slaveholder and his entire family. Armed with hatchets and knives, Turner and his men moved from plantation to plantation, slaughtering all whites they encountered. More than forty slaves joined him, taking their chance for freedom. Within twelve hours, Turner and his men had killed more than 50 whites, including women and children.

Local armed whites quickly formed a militia and, backed by federal troops from nearby Fort Monroe, crushed the rebellion. Turner and his men retreated into the woods, but white mobs retaliated, slaying blacks, many whom had nothing to do

Woodcut of Nat Turner (likely holding sword) and some of his companions, which would have appeared in the newspaper during the period of his imprisonment and trial (Oct. 30 –Nov. 11, 1831). It depicts the slaying of Turner's slave owner Mr. Travis (2) and other Southampton County, VA whites begging for their lives. The Nat Turner Rebellion struck fear into Southern slaveholders' hearts and resulted in increased restrictions on slaves and free blacks as well.

with the revolt.

Turner eluded capture for two months, adding to the lore that he had mystical powers, yet on October 30, 1831, a white farmer discovered his hiding place. Turner surrendered peacefully, and he was held in the South Hampton County Jail. He told his story—his "confessions"—to Thomas Gray who interviewed him from his prison cell. Turner and 55 others were executed.

Following Turner's insurrection, Virginia tightened its grip on the enslaved as well as on free blacks, forbidding preaching by free and enslaved blacks as well as assembling to teach blacks to read or write.

The Amistad Revolt

led to one of th[e] most celebrated trials involving the slav[e] trade. Thirty-five Africans of the Mend[e] people won their freedom and returne[d] to their home, Sierra Leone.

In 1839, Portuguese slave trade[rs] bargained for 110 Africans and trans[s]ported them illegally to Cuba where the[y] were sold to Spanish traders. Fifty-thre[e] of those Africans, led by Sengbe Pie[h] known as Cinque, revolted while bein[g] forcibly transported to sugar plantation[s] on the island. They killed the captain o[f] the ship La Amistad and several cre[w] members. The Africans spared the live[s] of two crew members and demande[d] that they return them to Africa. The du[o] navigated the ship toward Africa by da[y] but toward U.S. waters by night.

La Amistad was seized off the coas[t] of Long Island, New York. The African[s] were taken to New London, Connecticu[t] charged with murder and mutiny, an[d] then imprisoned to await trial in Har[t]ford, Connecticut. This took place thre[e] decades after Great Britain and the U.[S.] Constitution had outlawed the impor[t]ing of slaves. Outraged by the captive[s] imprisonment, abolitionists quickl[y] mobilized. Lewis Tappan, Joshua Levit[t] and Simon Jocelyn, formed the Amista[d] Committee to support the Africans.

They arranged to pay legal expense[s] for the Africans and promptly publicize[d] their plight in an "Appeal to the Friend[s] of Liberty." Tappan maneuvered adeptl[y]

Artwork that likely appeared in the newspaper when the African captives from the Amistad *were awaiting trial in Hartford, Connecticut, July 1839. Those on both sides of the slavery debate kept the issue before the public through the use of newspaper, magazine, and small pamphlets. This illustration, depicting the battle onboard* La Amistad, *as the Africans fought to take control, was clearly meant to illicit pro-slavery sentiment.*

behind the scenes, as well as boldly in the forefront, keeping the trial in the public eye and in the press. In a packed courtroom, the case went before Federal District Court Judge Andrew Judson, and the Africans told their story through an interpreter. Cinque served as their spokesman and said, as quoted in the New York Sun, "Brothers, we have done that which we proposed…I am resolved it is better to die than be a white man's slave."[68]

The defense argued that the mutiny was justified, as the Africans were free men captured in violation of international antislavery laws. This began a long series of court battles that went all the way to the Supreme Court.

In U.S. District Court, Judge Andrew Judson ruled that the Africans had mutinied to regain their freedom and ordered them freed and returned to Africa. Judson continued, noting that the Africans "were born free and ever since have been and still of right are free and not slaves." They revolted the ruling stated,

out of a natural "desire of winning their liberty and returning to their families."[69]

On appeal, the U.S. Circuit Court upheld the decision. Appealed again, the case was brought before the U.S. Supreme Court. John Quincy Adams, who would become sixth President of the United States, then serving in Congress, argued on behalf of the Africans. If the President could hand over free men on the demand of a foreign government, he questioned the court, how could any man, woman, and child in the United States ever be sure of their "blessing of freedom"? On March 9, 1841, the U.S. Supreme Court upheld the decision and ordered the return of the captives. Adams wrote to Tappan, "The captives are free! Thanks! In the name of humanity and justice, to you."[70]

In December 1841, 35 of the survivors prepared to return home, the others having died at sea or while in prison. Abolitionists provided a ship, and Tappan successfully recruited clergymen to accompany the Africans back to Sierra Le-

one. They arrived safely in January 1842.

Tappan received this first communication from the Africans, composed at sea near Sierra Leone:

Mr. Tappan—Dear Sir:

Captain good—no touch Mendi people. All Mendi people love Mr. Tappan. Mr. Tappan, pray for Cinque and all Mendi people all time, and Cinque and Mendi people pray for Mr. Tappan all time….Cinque love Mr. Tappan very much, and all Mendi people love Mr. Tappan very much. I no forget Mr. Tappan forever and ever; and I no forget God, because God help Mr. Tappan and Mendi people….I thank all 'merica people for they send Mendi people home. I shall never forget 'merica people.

Your friend, CINQUE[71]

The Amistad Case resulted in the freeing of these illegally transported Africans, but did not affect the status of the enslaved in America. Tappan and other abolitionists would continue to press for emancipation.

Abolitionist Armed Struggle

John Brown was born into a deeply Christian family in Torrington, Connecticut, in 1800, where state laws gradually abolishing slavery had begun in 1784, but full freedom for the enslaved would not occur until 1848. His father was vehemently opposed to slavery and, when Brown was five, moved the family to a district in northern Ohio that would become known for its anti-slavery views. Brown always worked for the abolition of slavery, but rose to the forefront of the movement in 1855 after he followed five of his sons to Bleeding Kansas. When violent pro-slavery forces burned the free black community of Lawrence, Kansas, Brown organized a militia that struck a bloody revenge.

Fed up with the pacifism of many abolitionists, Brown held a series of secret meetings with twelve whites and 34 blacks in Chatham, Ontario in May 1858 to plan the establishment of a revolutionary government of freed slaves. Chatham was the central settlement in Canada for escaped slaves from the United States. Six wealthy abolitionists backed Brown financially, with "no questions asked." Believing he had been chosen as an instrument

John Brown, the white abolitionist who led 21 men in an attack raid on the federal arsenal that produced muskets, rifles, pistols and other equipment for the United States military, is remembered for his dramatic, yet ill-fated attempt to arm the enslaved to rid the nation of the curse of slavery. John Brown's raid is credited as pivotal to the growing pressure for emancipation of the enslaved that brought the nation to the Civil War.

of God to overthrow the slave system, Brown and a multiracial group of like-minded men prepared to move forward with their plan. They needed weapons and decided to capture the federal arsenal at Harpers Ferry, Virginia. They would arm area slaves whom they thought would join in the fight. It was a daring venture. Frederick Douglass, whom Brown asked to join him, believed it doomed to fail.

Among the band were five black men, three free born and two former slaves. On October 16, 1859, they attacked Harpers Ferry—cut telegraph lines, captured the armory and succeeded in taking slave-

holders as hostages. When townsmen learned of the armed raid, they formed a militia and surrounded the armory, cutting off all possible escape routes. When word reached Washington, D.C., federal troops rushed in and squashed the attack. Casualties were minimal. During the 36-hour assault, Brown's men killed four and wounded nine; ten of Brown's men were killed; seven, including Brown, were captured.

Brown was found guilty of treason against Virginia and when he was hanged on December 2, 1859, many northern church bells tolled, acknowledging him as a martyr for freedom.

Black Men in Armed Struggle with John Brown

One of the five black Harpers Ferry raiders Osborn Perry Anderson escaped and remained free. He wrote an eyewitness account of the raid, so that his fallen black comrades would not be forgotten.

Osborn Perry Anderson

was born free in Pennsylvania in 1830, attended public schools, and according to some sources, also attended Oberlin College in Ohio. He left for Canada when the 1850 Fugitive Slave Act made life even more difficult not only for those who had escaped slavery, but also for those born free.

In Canada, Anderson worked as a printer for the abolitionist newspaper, *The Provincial Freeman*, and attended the Chatham Convention of May 1858, convened by Martin R. Delany

and John Brown to plan militant action to free slaves in the United States. He often served as secretary at such meetings but at this meeting stepped forward to fight with Brown at Harper's Ferry.

During the raid, Anderson helped to capture white slaveholders, among them the great-grand nephew of President George Washington. When federal soldiers advanced, and Brown surrendered, Anderson and a white comrade, Albert Hazlett, escaped. Hazlett was later captured, but Anderson, aided by Underground

Railroad agents, safely reached Canada.

Two years after the raid, Anderson published *A Voice from Harpers Ferry*, the only eyewitness account of the attack. His purpose for writing was "to save from oblivion the heroism of the colored men who so nobly seconded the efforts of the immortal John Brown."

Anderson returned to the U.S. and enlisted with the Union Army in 1864 where he served as a recruiter for black soldiers. Anderson lived until 1872.

Lewis Sheridan Leary

was born on March 17, 1835, to free parents in Fayetteville, North Carolina. His father John O'Leary was an Irishman; his mother was of African and American Indian descent. His father, a successful businessman, provided Leary and his siblings with a private education that included tutors and attendance at the free colored school in Fayetteville. Leary's privileged lifestyle in Fayetteville came to an end when he witnessed a white man beating a slave. He intervened, beating the white man. For his own safety, Leary had to flee the state.

He arrived in Oberlin, Ohio in 1857, where his sister and nephew, John Copeland lived.

At some point he dropped the

"O'" in his last name, and became known as Leary. He attended Oberlin College and supported himself by designing and making saddles, a trade learned from his father. Leary married a free black woman and they had one child. He also became actively involved in the Oberlin Anti-Slavery Society and participated in the Oberlin-Wellington Rescue of John Price, a runaway slave whom federal authorities tried to capture under the 1850 Fugitive Slave Act. Leary and others helped Price escape to Canada.

That same year, 1858, Leary and his nephew John Copeland were invited to meet John Brown and, after

a lengthy discussion, agreed to join Brown's raid. At Harpers Ferry, Leary and two other men were assigned to seize a rifle works. Surrounded by militia, cut off from the others, the three men fled. Leary was shot and captured by federal troops. He survived eight agonizing hours before succumbing to his wounds.

Leary was able to send a message to his wife, who did not know of his plans when he left her and their six-month-old child to follow Brown, reportedly saying, "I am ready to die." His widow received his bloodstained cape that he wore during the raid. The connection between Leary and abolitionists continued, for abolitionists James Redpath and Wendell Phillips educated Leary's child.

John Copeland was born free in Raleigh, North Carolina in 1834 and moved to Oberlin, Ohio in 1842. He graduated from Oberlin College, an institution known for abolition fervor. In 1858, Copeland participated in the Oberlin-Wellington rescue of John Price, a runaway slave whom federal authorities tried to capture under the 1850 Fugitive Slave Act. Copeland and others helped Price escape to Canada.

His uncle, Lewis Sheridan Leary, recruited Copeland to join him in the John Brown raid. Copeland's role had been to seize control of Hall's Rifle Works. He was captured, found guilty and sentenced to death. Copeland was hanged December 16, 1859 but while awaiting execution, Copeland wrote to his parents telling them why he took part in the raid and making his peace with God. In part, the letter stated:

...Dear Parents, my fate so far as man can seal it, is sealed, but let not this fact occasion you any misery; for remember the cause in which I was engaged, remember it as a holy cause, one in which men in every way better than I am, have suffered & died. Remember that if I must die, I die in-trying to liberate a few of my poor & oppressed people from a condition of servitude against which God in his word has hurled his most bitter denunciations, a cause in which men, who though removed from its direct injurious effects by the color of their faces have already lost their lives, & more yet must meet the fate which man has decided I must meet. If die I must, I shall try to meet my fate as a man who can suffer in the glorious cause in which I have been engaged, without a groan, & meet my Maker in heaven as a christian man who through the saving grace of God has made his peace with Him. [72]

Dangerfield Newby

Born in 1815 in Fauquier County, Virginia, Dangerfield Newby was the child of a white slave owner and an enslaved black woman. In 1858 Newby's master moved to Ohio, and was required by law to free his slaves. Although Newby was free, his wife, Harriet, and their children remained enslaved in Virginia. Harriet would write him, urging him to hurry and purchase the family. The slaveholder who owned her needed the money and she did not know if he would wait much longer before selling Newby's family. Newby raised $725 to free her and his youngest child, but the slave owner raised the purchase price. Unable to purchase his family's freedom, Newby joined John Brown, hoping the insurrection would free his wife and other enslaved blacks. Newby was the first of Brown's men to die in the attack on Harpers Ferry. Letters from Newby's wife were found on him at the time of his death. On August 16, 1859 she wrote:

Shields Green (Greene), known as the Emperor to the Harpers Ferry raiders was born enslaved in Charleston, South Carolina, around 1836, he escaped, spent time in Rochester, New York, and in Oberlin, Ohio and became active in the abolition movement. Frederick Douglass introduced him to John Brown. Douglass wrote:

While at my house, John Brown made the acquaintance Negro man who called himself by different names-sometimes "Emperor," at other times, "Shields Green." He was a fugitive slave, who had made his escape from Charleston, South Carolina; a State from which a slave found it no easy matter to run away. But Shields Green was not one to shrink from hardships or dangers. He was a man of few words, and his speech was singularly broken; but his courage and self-respect made him quite a dignified character. John Brown saw at once what "stuff" Green "was made of," and confided to him his plans and purposes. Green easily believed in Brown, and promised to go with him whenever he should be ready to move.

.. When I found that he [Brown] had fully made up his mind and could not be dissuaded, I turned to Shields Green and told him he heard what Captain Brown had said; his old plan was changed, and that I should return home, and if he wished to go with me he could do so. Captain Brown urged us both to go with him, but I could not do so, and could but feel that he was about to rivet the fetters more firmly than ever on the limbs of the enslaved…

…When about to leave I asked Green what he had decided to do, and was surprised by his coolly saying, in his broken way, "I b'leve I'll go wid de ole man."[73]

According to Douglass, during the raid one of Brown's men escaped and later told him that Green could have escaped also. Green instead decided to stand with Brown, even unto death. On the day of Brown's execution, Green sent word to him, saying he was glad to have fought with him and awaited his execution willingly.

Dear Husband:
…I want you to buy me as soon as possible for if you do not get me somebody else will the servants are very disagreeable they do all they can to set my mistress against me Dear Husband you not the trouble I see the last two years has ben like a troubled dream to me it is said Master is in want of money if so I know not what time he may sell me an then all my bright hops of the futer are blasted for there has ben one bright hope to cheer me in all my troubles that is to be with you for if I thought I shoul never see you this earth would have no charms fo me do all you Can for me, witch I have no doubt you will. I want to see you so much the Chrildren are all well the baby cannot walk yet all it can step around enny thing by holding on it is very much like Agnes I mus bring my letter to Close as I have no newes to write you mus write soon and say when you think you can Come.

Your Affectionate Wife[74]
Harriet Newby

Newby's family was later sold to planters in Louisiana. Dangerfield Newby's brother William continued the fight for freedom, serving in the 5th U.S. Colored Troops in the Civil War. William Newby died at Petersburg in June 1864.[75]

45

Efforts to Uphold, Enforce & Justify Slavery

Henry Clay introduces the Compromise of 1850 in the Senate. When it became law, California was admitted to the Union a free state, but in exchange the Fugitive Slave Law was passed, which required northerners to return runaway slaves to their owners under penalty of law.

The combination of emancipation and manumission efforts were met by those determined to uphold, enforce and justify slavery.

Antislavery societies and organizations to resettle newly freed blacks faced an uphill battle against the illegal Trans-Atlantic slave trade, which continued nearly until the Civil War.

Rebellion by enslaved blacks against slave holders was answered with brutal force, harsher restrictions and punishing consequences.

Brave individuals in the Underground Railroad helped escaped slaves, but slave catchers and federal martials pursued and recaptured them, often kidnapping free born or manumitted blacks.

Abolitionists fought court battles, like the famous Amistad and Dred Scott cases. Pro-slavery lawyers, funded by the wealth slavery generated, opposed them and appealed their victorious rulings, making the legal process long and expensive.

While legislators passed laws like The Northwest Ordinance that forbade slavery in what is now the Midwest, the conflict about slavery arose again as each new territory was added to U.S. westward expansion. Because the Constitution counted a portion of the slave population to determine Congressional representation giving states with large slave populations a dispropor-

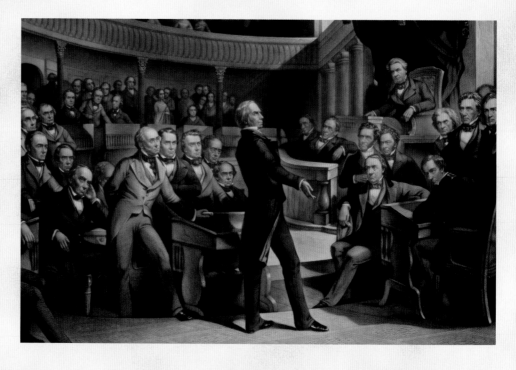

tionately greater number Congress-men, legislative advocates of slavery became powerful law makers and anti-slavery legislation blockers. In every addition of new territory, they forced compromise on slavery—the Missouri Compromise of 1820, the Compromise of 1850, the Kansas-Nebraska Act of 1854—blocking full freedom of blacks.

Pro-slavery forces, from plantation owners to elected officials to preach-ers argued that slavery was a moral institution, but they ultimately relied on the Constitution, into which those three tragically flawed clauses were written. When William Lloyd Garrison established the American Anti-Slavery Society, a primary target of his anti-slavery efforts was the U.S. Constitu-tion. He said, "We pronounce it the most bloody and heaven-daring ar-rangement ever made by men for the continuance and protection of a sys-tem of the most atrocious villany ever exhibited on earth."[76]

Those on the side of freedom faced the assumption of the times that Europeans were superior to people of other continents—Asia, North and South America, Australia and Africa—an attitude that made enslaving Afri-cans possible. The deeply ingrained culture of the founders of the United States was that freedom or liberty was meant for men of European de-scent. But despite the views of their era, some always believed slavery was a contradiction to the founding ideals of the United States. And those op-posed to slavery always met pro-slav-

According to the 1860 census, on a typical plantation (more than 20 slaves) the capi-tal value of the slaves was greater than the capital value of the land and implements.

ery resistance—legislative, judicial, coercive and violent--from the writ-ing of the Constitution until the 1850s when slavery become the issue in na-tional politics. That led to new means of maintaining slavery—breaking the bond of national unity and war.

Jefferson Davis, president of the Confederate States of America, said to his Confederate Congress on April 29, 1861 after the Southern states had se-ceded from the United States and fired the shots that had begun the Civil War:

…the African slaves had augmented in number from about 600,000, at the date of the adoption of the constitutional compact, to upward of 4,000,000. In moral and social condi-tion they had been elevated from brutal savages into docile, intelli-gent, and civilized agricultural labor-ers, and supplied not only with bodily comforts but with careful religious instruction. Under the supervision

of a superior race, their labor had been so directed as not only to allow a gradual and marked amelioration of their own condition, but to convert hundreds of thousands of square miles of the wilderness into cultivat-ed lands covered with a prosperous people; towns and cities had sprung into existence, and had rapidly increased in wealth and population under the social system of the South; … and the productions in the South of cotton, rice, sugar, and tobacco, for the full development and continu-ance of which the labor of African slaves was and is indispensable…[77]

On April 16, 1862, almost one year to the day after the attack on Fort Sum-ter which began the war, Jefferson Da-vis approved an act of the Confederate Congress that drafted—without ex-emption—every white male between ages of 18 and 35 for three years of military service.[78]

Slavery in National Politics Splits the Nation

Presidential candidates Abraham Lincoln, of the newly formed Republican Party, and Stephen A. Douglas, Democrat, are depicted in a footrace for the Capitol in this 1860 political cartoon. Slavery was a dividing issue, with Lincoln expressing his reservation about expansion of the institution early in the campaign. In addition to Stephen Douglas, two other candidates ran for president: John Bell of the Constitution Union Party and John Breckenridge from the Democratic Party South. Douglas was the candidate for the Democratic Party North after the party had split over slavery at its convention that year. Because of the four-way race, President Lincoln won the Electoral College with only 40 percent of the popular vote, and it was not surprising that he failed to carry even one slave-holding state.

During the 1850s, the issue of slavery dominated national politics in the U.S. Debates in Congress reflected the importance of slavery in politics. And as from the founding of nation, compromises were made on the practice of human bondage. The Compromise of 1850 allowed California to enter the Union as a free state and outlawed slave trading in the District of Columbia, but it also strengthened the Fugitive Slave Act. The Kansas-Nebraska Act of 1854 opened new lands as U.S. territories, allowing white settlers to decide whether they would prohibit or allow slavery. This was viewed as a setback for those on the side of freedom because Kansas had been officially closed to slavery for more than thirty years, since a previous effort to find middle ground on slavery, the Missouri Compromise of 1820.

Political parties were affected as well. The U.S. had not yet become a two-party political system. Key political parties included Whig, Democrat, Constitutional Union and American. Men who were against the expansion of slavery, many of whom advocated abolition, formed the Republican Party. It became known as the antislavery party. It countered the Democratic Party which was seen as advocating the interests of slaveholders. In 1854, newspaper publisher Horace Greeley stated about a new party:

We should not care much whether those thus united (against slavery) were designated 'Whig,' 'Free Democrat' or something else; though we think some simple name like 'Republican' would more fitly designate those who had united to restore the Union to its true mission of champion and promulgator of Liberty rather than propagandist of slavery. [79]

In 1856 the Republican Party ran its first presidential candidate, western explorer John C. Fremont who ran against Democrat James Buchanan and American Party candidate Willard Fillmore. Fremont lost to Buchanan only by approximately 500,000 votes and 60 electoral college votes. [80]

Two years later in 1858, the party gained national visibility in the Illinois Senate race when the well-known incumbent, Stephen Douglas (who had crafted the Kansas–Nebraska Act of 1854) campaigned against Abraham Lincoln, a former Congressman who had only served one term in the legislature.

Accepting the Republican Party's Senate nomination Lincoln said, quoting the Bible: " 'A house divided against itself cannot stand.' I believe this Government cannot endure permanently half-slave and half-free." He was expressing his belief that slavery would be able to spread to northern states because of the 1854 Kansas-Nebraska Act and the 1857 Dred Scott decision (in which the Supreme Court decided that Congress did not have the right to exclude slavery from a territory).

The campaign included a series of seven debates between the two candidates and slavery was a common issue discussed.

Lincoln's reservations regarding slavery were expressed in the very first debate. [81]

This declared indifference, but, as I must think, covert real zeal for the spread of slavery, I cannot but hate. I hate it because of the monstrous injustice of slavery itself. I hate it because it deprives our republican example of its just influence in the world; enables the enemies of free institutions, with plausibility, to taunt us as hypocrites; causes the real friends of freedom to doubt our sincerity, and especially because it forces so many really good men amongst ourselves into an open war with the very fundamental principles of civil liberty - criticizing the Declaration of Independence, and insisting that there is no right principle of action but self-interest. [82]

In the debate, Douglas' attempted to occupy a middle ground between pro- and anti-slavery advocates, appealing to both. He appealed to the belief of black inferiority held by most southerners and many northerners, while also implicitly suggesting that both regions had the right to determine whether the institution of slavery was appropriate for their areas: *For thousands of years the negro has been a race upon the earth, and during all that time, in all latitudes and climates, wherever he has wandered or been taken, he has been inferior to the race which he has there met. He belongs to an inferior race, and must always occupy an inferior position. I do not hold that because the negro is our inferior therefore he ought to be a slave. By no means can such a conclusion be drawn from what I have said. On the contrary, I hold that humanity and Christianity both require that the negro shall have and enjoy every right, every privilege, and every immunity consistent with the safety of the society in which he lives.*[83]

Lincoln lost the election but he returned to politics in 1860 as the Republican candidate for president. By that time, the 1859 attack on Harpers Ferry was still a fresh memory resulting in radical antislavery sentiment, social pressure by antislavery societies was growing, and publications like *Uncle Tom's Cabin* had an incalculable cultural influence. The country was so divided on the issue of slavery that the Democratic Party split into a northern and southern party. Lincoln ran against John Bell (The Constitutional Union Party), John Breckenridge (Democratic Party South) , and Stephen Douglas (Democratic Party North). The Republican Party was not even on the ballot in the South. Lincoln won with 180 electoral votes and 1.9 million popular votes. [84]

From Secession to Rebellion to War

Abraham Lincoln did not advocate an immediate end to slavery. He stated that he believed slavery was wrong and that he was against the spread of slavery to new U.S. territories.

Many southerners felt slavery could only continue to exist if it could expand. And only if slavery survived, would they

This image published December 1, 1860, in Frank Leslie's Illustrated newspaper, shows an enthusiastic secession meeting at Mills House in Charleston, SC. On December 20, 1860, state delegates met in Columbia and voted unanimously to secede. South Carolina, a state with four signers of the United States Constitution, became the first state to leave the Union over the dividing issue of slavery.

continue to reap economic benefits. Southerners saw the election of Lincoln—the northerner who did not agree with them on the expansion of slavery—as the empowering of an enemy who would soon have control over them when he was inaugurated in March of 1861 (the standard inauguration date in that era). [85]

In December 1860, a month after the election of Lincoln, South Carolina legislators met and voted overwhelmingly to secede, or leave the Union. During the next few months other legislative bodies in southern states also voted to leave the Union. By the time Abraham Lincoln was inaugurated in March of 1861, the seceding states had joined together to create a new country, the Confederate States of America (C.S.A.). Their representatives wrote a new constitution which affirmed slavery, elected Virginian Jefferson Davis as their president, and selected Richmond, Virginia as

the capital.

In his inaugural address, Lincoln expressed interest in reconciliation with the Confederate states. During his first month in office he reached out to convince the states that had left the Union that it was not possible to do so. He tried to persuade the four slave states that had not left the union, Maryland, Delaware, Kentucky, and Missouri, to remain in the Union. [86]

When states left the Union, property that had been owned by the federal government based in Washington, D.C. was in dispute. The federal army outpost Fort Sumter on an island off the coast of Charleston, South Carolina, remained under control of Union troops. In April, supplies began running out. Confederate leaders notified President Lincoln that an attempt to resupply the fort would be viewed as an aggressive act, and that they would resist such Union efforts. Had Lincoln conceded to the

Confederates, he would have affirmed Confederate power. Confederate troops were unsuccessful in their attempts to get the Union soldiers at the Fort to surrender before supplies arrived. Early on the morning of April 12, 1861, Confederate ships began firing at the fort. After thirty-one hours of shelling, the Fort was destroyed and the Union soldiers surrendered.

When President Lincoln received the news, he declared a state of rebellion and issued a call to the states that remained in the Union to provide 75,000 troops. (The army at this time was a small all-volunteer army.) The Civil War had begun.[87]

In April 1861 the Northern states had a much greater population, an extensive railroad network, and a well developed system of factories capable of producing a range of products. The Confederate states had many fewer citizens (a substantial portion of their number was enslaved), were primarily farm economies, and had very limited industries. The assumption among Northerners was that the conflict would be short, that the Union would be swiftly victorious. The Confederate states, however, had strong military leadership, and most of the battles were fought on familiar terrain in the South. In the two first years of the war, the Union Army struggled. Abraham Lincoln changed commanders several times, but they still struggled.[88]

Lincoln, as well as many white Northerners, explained the purpose of the war was to preserve the unity of the nation. Once part of the United States, a

Fugitive African Americans forged the Rappahannock River in Virginia in August 1862 into land controlled by the Union Army, which, to them, meant freedom from slavery and protection from re-enslavement. Once on Union soil, however, slaves were considered "Contrabands"—property of War. During this period their status as free people was uncertain. Contraband camps developed around Union forts and encampments. The manual labor of such fugitives was used to aid the war effort.

state could never leave. If the Confederate States were allowed to secede, other states might leave at some later date. Denying the southern states to ability to leave, these advocates believed the United States would remain intact in the future.

By contrast, most African Americans, those enslaved and free, saw the war as a battle for Black freedom. As soon as war broke out, enslaved African Americans began to escape, finding their way to Union troops. Initially Union forces sent escapees back to slaveholders. Eventually the Union leaders realized that by sending enslaved African Americans back, they were helping the enemy to raise food and other products that could be used by Confederate soldiers against the Union Army. In 1861 General

Benjamin Butler suggested a change in the policy and recommended that enslaved African Americans who managed to reach Union camps be treated as "contraband of war" and granted their freedom.

Although many of the enslaved remained on plantations, as the war progressed the numbers fleeing to freedom increased. Wherever the Union Army camped, large groups of formerly enslaved African Americans typically formed nearby. Known as "contraband camps", these camps were the first taste of nominal freedom for many blacks. Despite danger, those on the side of freedom—whites and African American—volunteered to travel from the North to teach in contraband camp schools and provide other assistance.[89]

The Confederate attack

on Fort Sumter on April 12, 1861, marked the start of the Civil War. But the rebellion was not quickly squashed, as Lincoln and most in the North had anticipated. More than a year later, bloody battles continued in what is still the deadliest war in terms of soldier casualties in U.S. history.

A lot has been documented about the Civil War in books and films and other media. The causes of the conflict are still debated by historians, yet most agree that the war was fought by the North to preserve the unity of the country, and by the South to break it apart.

Only blacks—enslaved and free— and perhaps ardent abolitionists would have argued that freeing the slaves was the reason the Civil War was fought. Frederick Douglass, in an Independence Day speech on July 4, 1862, observed:

"It is hardly necessary at this very late day of the war . . . to enter now upon any elaborate enquiry or explanation as to whence came the foul and guilty attempt to break up and destroy the national Government. All but the willfully blind or the malignantly traitorous, know and confess that this whole movement which now so largely distracts the country, and threatens ruin to the nation, has its root and its sap, its trunk and its branches, and the bloody fruit it bears only from the one source of all abounding abomination,

War

The Battle of Antietam, fought September 17, 1862, was the bloodiest, single-day battle in American history, with casualties from both sides totaling 23,000. Dead soldiers are piled in front of a wagon on the battlefield, and in the background is Dunker Church, used by the Confederate Army as a medical station and after the battle by the Union as an embalming station. President Lincoln was awaiting a Union victory before issuing his order for freedom. On September 22, 1862, five days after Union victory at Antietam, Lincoln issued his Preliminary Emancipation Proclamation, which would effect freedom on January 1, 1863 for the enslaved in the Confederacy if those states did not cease their rebellion.

and that is slavery. It has sprung out of a malign selfishness and a haughty and imperious pride which only the practice of the most hateful oppression and cruelty could generate and develop. No ordinary love of gain, nor ordinary love of power, could have stirred up this terrible revolt. . . .

There is . . . one false theory of the origin of the war to which a moment's reply may be properly given here. It is this. The abolitionists by their insane and unconstitutional attempt to abolish slavery have brought on the war. . . . In answer to this charge, I lay down this rule as a basis to which all candid men will assent. Whatever is said or done by any class of citizens, strictly in accordance with rights guaranteed by the Constitution, cannot be fairly charged as against the Union, or as inciting to a dissolution of the Union.

Now the slaveholders came into the Union with their eyes wide open, subject to a Constitution wherein the right to be abolitionists was sacredly guaranteed to all the people. They knew that slavery was to take its chance with all other evils against the power of free speech, and national enlightenment. They came on board the national ship subject to these conditions, they signed the articles after having duly read them, and the fact that those rights, plainly written, have been exercised is no apology whatever for the slaveholder's mutiny and their attempt to lay piratical hands on the ship and its officers. When therefore I hear a man denouncing abolitionists on account of the war, I know that I am listening to a man who either does not know what he is talking about, or to one who is a traitor in disguise."[90]

The Civil War was not fought to free enslaved blacks, but it resulted

Casualties of Kimball's Brigade during the Battle of Antietam are tossed in a nearby ditch. The dead lay scattered across battlefields and in trenches throughout the Civil War. Their remains often were later interred in a mass grave.

in freedom. It prompted freedom for enslaved blacks in the United States. It was the bloody conflict that gave President Lincoln the power of wartime commander-in-chief, the tactical resources, the resolve and the opportunity to free the enslaved under intense pressure from abolitionists and military forces.

In August 1861, less than six months after the outbreak of the Civil War, Congress passed The Confiscation Act which Lincoln signed. The law gave the government ownership of property—including enslaved blacks—used to support the Confederate war effort. The act stripped slaveowners of claims to their human property, but did not declare the slaves free.[91]

Union military commanders also pressured the President to free the slaves. During war, enemy property was confiscated by soldiers, so in battle areas slaves taken by Union forces became the property of the U.S. government. General David Hunter, a Union Army commander of Georgia, South Carolina and Florida issued an order in May of 1862, freeing all slaves in areas under his command. Lincoln rescinded this order, saying military leaders did not have the authority to free slaves.[92]

Enslaved blacks in conquered Confederate territories, briefly freed by Hunter's military command, were again deemed property, and now the property of the federal government. This only added more confusion and increased pressure on Lincoln to emancipate.

By the summer of 1862, the Union Army had better leadership, but the end of the war was still not in sight. The military had not achieved decisive victory that would compel the Confederate States to rejoin the United States. President Lincoln decided to try to pressure the Confederacy by threatening the institution that they most wanted to preserve—slavery.

In July 1862, Lincoln secretly discussed an executive order emancipating the slaves with his cabinet for the first time. However, he was concerned that it would appear to be an act of desperation by the Commander-in-Chief of a losing Union Army; he would wait to announce the order until the Union Army had a decisive victory on the battlefield to back it up with military strength.

Abolitionists, who had been pressing for emancipation for some fifty years, grew impatient with Lincoln as clearly stated in an editorial published in August 1862, by Horace Greeley, the editor of the widely read *New York Tribune*. In the acclaimed open letter on behalf of the population of the North, "The Prayer of Twenty Millions," Greeley wrote of the specific plight of enslaved blacks as the war was fought.

To ABRAHAM LINCOLN, President of the United States

DEAR SIR: I do not intrude to tell you--for you must know already--that a great proportion of those who triumphed in your election…are sorely disappointed and deeply pained by the policy you seem to be pursuing with regard to the slaves of the Rebels.

… We think you are strangely and disastrously remiss in the discharge of your official and imperative duty with regard to the emancipating provisions of the new Confiscation Act. Those provisions were designed to fight Slavery with Liberty. They prescribe that men loyal to the Union, and willing to shed their blood in her behalf, shall no longer be held, with the Nations consent, in bondage to persistent, malignant traitors, who for twenty years have been plotting and for sixteen months have been fighting to divide and destroy our country. Why these traitors should be treated with tenderness by you, to the prejudice of the dearest rights of loyal men, We cannot conceive.

… We ask you to consider that Slavery is everywhere the inciting cause and sustaining base of treason.

… We complain that the Union cause has suffered, and is now suffering immensely, from mistaken deference to Rebel Slavery… The Rebels from the first have been eager to confiscate, imprison, scourge and kill: we have fought wolves with the devices of sheep.

We complain that the Confiscation Act which you approved is habitually disregarded by your Generals, and that no word of rebuke for them from you has yet reached the public ear. Fremont's Proclamation and Hunter's Order favoring Emancipation were promptly annulled by you; while Halleck's No. 3, forbidding fugitives from Slavery to Rebels to come within his lines—an order as unmilitary as inhuman, and which received the hearty approbation of every traitor in America—with scores of like tendency, have never provoked even your own remonstrance. We complain that the officers of your Armies have habitually repelled rather than invited approach of slaves who would have gladly taken the risks of escaping from their Rebel masters to our camps, bringing intelligence often of inestimable value to the Union cause. We complain that those who have thus escaped to us, avowing a willingness to do for us whatever might be required, have been brutally and madly repulsed, and often surrendered to be scourged, maimed and tortured by the ruffian traitors, who pretend to own them. We complain that a large proportion of our regular Army Officers, with many of the Volunteers, evince far more solicitude to uphold Slavery than to put down the Rebellion. And finally, we complain that you, Mr. President, elected as a Republican, knowing well what an abomination Slavery is, and how emphatically it is the core and essence of this atrocious Rebellion, seem never to interfere with these atrocities, and never give a direction to your Military subordinates, which does not appear to have been conceived in the interest of Slavery rather than of Freedom.

Let me call your attention to the recent tragedy in New Orleans, whereof the facts are obtained entirely through Pro-Slavery channels. A considerable body of resolute, able-bodied men, held in Slavery by two Rebel sugar-planters in defiance of the Confiscation Act which you have approved, left plantations thirty miles distant and made their way to the great mart of the South-West, which they knew to be the indisputed possession of the Union forces. They made their way safely and quietly through thirty miles of Rebel territory, expecting to find freedom under the protection of our flag. Whether they had or had not heard of the passage of the Confiscation Act, they reasoned logically that we could not kill them for deserting the service of their lifelong oppressors, who had through treason become our implacable enemies. They came to us for liberty and protection, for which they were willing render their best service: they met with hostility, captivity, and murder. The barking of the base curs of Slavery in this quarter deceives no one—not even themselves. They say, indeed, that the negroes had no right to appear in New Orleans armed (with their implements of daily labor in the cane-field); but no one doubts that they would gladly have laid these down if assured that they should be free. They were set upon and maimed, captured and killed, because they sought the benefit of that act of Congress which they may not specifically have heard of, but which was none the less the law of the land which they had a clear right to the benefit of—which it was somebody's duty to publish far and wide, in order that so many as possible should be impelled to desist from serving Rebels and the Rebellion and come over to the side of the Union, They sought their liberty in strict accordance with the law of the land—they were butchered or re-enslaved for so doing by the help of Union soldiers enlisted to fight against slaveholding Treason. It was somebody's fault that they were so murdered—if others shall hereafter stuffer in like manner, in default of explicit and public directions to your generals that they are to recognize and obey the Confiscation Act, the world will lay the blame on you. Whether you will choose to hear it through future History and 'at the bar of God, I will not judge. I can only hope.

… I close as I began with the statement that what an immense majority of the Loyal Millions of your countrymen require of you is a frank, declared, unqualified, ungrudging execution of the laws of the land, more especially of the Confiscation Act. That Act gives freedom to the slaves of Rebels coming within our lines, or whom those lines may at any time inclose--we ask you to render it due obedience by publicly requiring all your subordinates to recognize and obey it. The rebels are everywhere using the late anti-negro riots in the North, as they have long used your officers' treatment of negroes in the South, to convince the slaves that they have nothing to hope from a Union success-that we mean in that case to sell them into a bitter bondage to defray the cost of war. Let them impress this as a truth on the great mass of their ignorant and credulous bondsmen, and the Union will never be restored-never. We cannot conquer Ten Millions of People united in solid phalanx against us, powerfully aided by the Northern sympathizers and European allies. We must have scouts, guides, spies, cooks, teamsters, diggers and choppers from the Blacks of the South, whether we allow them to fight for us or not, or we shall be baffled and repelled. As one of the millions who would gladly have avoided this struggle at any sacrifice but that Principle and Honor, but who now feel that the triumph of the Union is dispensable not only to the existence of our country to the well being of mankind, I entreat you to render a hearty and unequivocal obedience to the law of the land.

Yours,
Horace Greeley
New York, August 19, 1862 [93]

Alexandria National Cemetery, established in 1862 in Virginia, served as burial grounds for Union soldiers who died in hospitals around the Alexandria area. Thousands died in tents or overcrowded, disease-ridden hospitals, where surgeries were performed with no anesthesia. A small site of 5.5 acres, it was almost filled to capacity by 1864, leading to the creation of Arlington National Cemetery.

Executive Mansion,
Washington, August 22, 1862

Hon. Horace Greeley:

*Dear Sir. I have just read yours of the 19th addressed to myself through **The New York Tribune**. If there be in it any statements, or assumptions of fact, which I may know to be erroneous, I do not, now and here, controvert them. If there be perceptable in it an impatient and dictatorial tone, I waive it in deference to an old friend, whose heart I have always supposed to be right.*

As to the policy I "seem to be pursuing" as you say, I have not meant to leave any one in doubt.

I would save the Union. I would save it the shortest way under the Constitution. The sooner the national authority can be restored; the nearer the Union will be "the Union as it was." If there be those who would not save the Union, unless they could at the same time save slavery, I do not agree with them. If there be those who would not save the Union unless they could at the same time destroy slavery, I do not agree with them. My paramount object in this struggle is to save the Union, and is not either to save or to destroy slavery. If I could save the Union without freeing any slave I would do it, and if I could save it by freeing all slaves I would do it; and if I could save it by freeing some and leaving others alone I would also do that. What I do about slavery, and the colored race, I do because I believe it helps to save the Union; and what I forbear, I forbear because I don't believe it would help to save the Union. I shall do less whenever I shall believe what I am doing hurts the cause, and I shall do more whenever I shall believe doing more will help the cause. I shall try to correct errors when shown to be error; and I shall adopt new views so fast as they shall appear to be true views.

I have here stated my purpose according to my view of Official duty: and I intend no modification of my oft-expressed personal wish that all men everywhere could be free.

Yours,

A. Lincoln [94]

Despite pressure from Congress, his military commanders and the abolitionists who voted him into office, Lincoln refused to reveal his plans before he had the military victory that would give his emancipation order clout. His reply to Greeley is the now-famous letter that convinced many that Lincoln was not sincere in his desire to free blacks, and that he subordinated his belief that slavery was morally wrong to his desire to bring the Confederate states back into the Union.

The Union victory in the Battle of Antietam provided Lincoln with an opportunity to provide those of African descent in the U.S. what the founders of the country had not in the Declaration of Independence, what the drafters of Constitution had specifically denied them, and what many legislative compromises failed to achieve—freedom.

But that freedom was provisional, and could only be achieved, if at all, by an orderly process. The Constitution which affirmed slavery in the U.S., was adopted on September 17, 1787, by the Constitutional Convention, but did not go into effect until March 4, 1789, after it was ratified by conventions in eleven states. [95]

Emancipation for the four million descendants of those six hundred thousand Africans, who were in bondage on U.S. soil when the Constitution was framed, was a lengthy process. Seventy-five years later, Lincoln's proposal was still rejected by the eleven states of the Confederacy.

The magnitude of the Civil War in U.S. lives is staggering. More than 600,000 died. According to the 1860 census the total U.S. population was 31,443,000. Consider that roughly a fifth of the total—six million—were young men old enough to fight, which would mean ten percent of the entire U.S. population of young men were killed in the prime of life in the Civil War. By comparison, about 60,000 U.S. servicemen died in Vietnam; about 120,000 U.S. military deaths in World War I; and about 400,000 U.S. soldiers in World War II, even though in each of those wars the population was greater than it had been during the Civil War.

Preliminary
Emancipation Proclamation

The entire presidency of Abraham Lincoln was a time of war and division. The burden shows on his face in this iconic image. Lincoln drafted the Preliminary Emancipation Proclamation in his own handwriting. (The images here are of the final copy preserved in the National Archives. To view Lincoln's handwritten draft visit www.nysm.nysed.gov/ep) A deeply thoughtful man, Lincoln was certain the Constitution gave the chief executive power to preserve the union, but did not believe it gave the president the authority to abolish slavery. Emancipation as his wartime measure would both begin the process of ending slavery and serve to preserve the union.

Lincoln waited until the Union victory at Antietam Creek in Maryland and five days later issued his offer, known as The Preliminary Emancipation Proclamation, on September 22, 1862. It stated that if the Confederates states returned to the Union within 100 days, they could resume being part of the Union with no threat to the institution of slavery. If they did not, then on January 1, 1863, all slaves in the territory that was then in rebellion would be forever free.

September 22, 1862
A Transcription

By the President of the United States of America.
A Proclamation.
I, Abraham Lincoln, President of the United States of America, and Commander-in-Chief of the Army and Navy thereof, do hereby proclaim and declare that hereafter, as heretofore, the war will be prosecuted for the object of practically restoring the constitutional relation between the United States, and each of the States, and the people thereof, in which States that relation is, or may be, suspended or disturbed.
Lincoln states the goal of the war is to forcibly bring the states back together.

That it is my purpose, upon the next meeting of Congress to again recommend the adoption of a practical measure tendering pecuniary aid to the free acceptance or rejection of all slave States, so called, the people whereof may not then be in rebellion against the United States and which States

may then have voluntarily adopted, or thereafter may voluntarily adopt, immediate or gradual abolishment of slavery within their respective limits; and that the effort
Slaveholders in states that are not part of the Confederacy will be compensated for freeing their slaves and may on their own immediately or gradually free those they hold in bondage.

to colonize persons of African descent, with their consent, upon this continent, or elsewhere, with the previously obtained consent of the Governments existing there, will be continued.

The government consents to freed blacks leaving the U.S. if they desire to go and if the governments where they wish to go will accept them.

That on the first day of January in the year of our Lord, one thousand eight hundred and sixty-three, all persons held as slaves within any State, or designated part of a State, the people whereof shall then be in rebellion against the United States shall be then, thenceforward, and forever free; and the executive government of the United States, including the military and naval authority thereof, will recognize and maintain the freedom of such persons, and will do no act or acts to repress such persons, or any of them, in any efforts they may make for their actual freedom.

This key clause declares that on 1/1/1863 slaves in the Confederate states that remain at war, will be free. The government and military will recognize their freedom, maintain their freedom, make no effort to deprive them of their freedom or hinder their own freedom efforts.

That the executive will, on the first day of January aforesaid, by proclamation, designate the States, and part of States, if any, in which the people thereof respectively, shall then be in rebellion against the United States; and the fact that any State, or the people thereof shall, on that day be, in good faith represented in the Congress of the United States, by members chosen thereto, at elections wherein a majority of the qualified voters of such State shall have participated, shall, in the absence of strong countervailing testimony, be deemed conclusive evidence that such State and the people thereof, are not then in rebellion against the United States.

States who send representatives to Congress by 1/1/1863 will be considered part of the U.S. and not the Confederacy. Those in bondage to them remain recognized as their property. In other words, if a Confederate state returns to the Union, they can continue slavery in their state.

That attention is hereby called to an Act of Congress entitled "An Act to make an additional Article of War" approved March 13, 1862, and which act is in the words and figure following:

"Be it enacted by the Senate and House of Representatives of the United States of America in Congress assembled, That hereafter the following shall be promulgated as an additional article of war for the government of the army of the United States, and shall be obeyed and observed as such:

"Article-All officers or persons in the military or naval service of the United States are prohibited from employing any of the forces under their respective commands for the purpose of returning fugitives from service or labor, who may have escaped from any persons to whom such service or labor is claimed to be due, and any officer who shall be found guilty by a court martial of violating this article shall be dismissed from the service.

"Sec.2. And be it further enacted, That this act shall take effect from and after its passage."

Also to the ninth and tenth sections of an act entitled "An Act to suppress Insurrection, to punish Treason and Rebellion, to seize and confiscate property of rebels, and for other purposes," approved July 17, 1862, and which sections are in the words and figures following:

"Sec.9. And be it further enacted, That all slaves of persons who shall hereafter be engaged in rebellion against the government of the United States, or who shall in any way give aid or comfort thereto, escaping from such persons and taking refuge within the lines of the army; and all slaves captured from such persons or deserted by them and coming under the control of the government of the United States; and all slaves of such persons found on (or) being within any place occupied

by rebel forces and afterwards occupied
by the forces of the United States, shall be
deemed captives of war, and shall be forever
free of their servitude and not again held as
slaves.

*This changes a previous law and says blacks
enslaved by Confederates in areas controlled
by Union soldiers or who escape to such areas
are free and will not be returned to slavery.*

"Sec.10. And be it further enacted, That no
slave escaping into any State, Territory, or
the District of Columbia, from any other
State, shall be delivered up, or in any way
impeded or hindered of his liberty, except
for crime, or some offence against the laws,
unless the person claiming said fugitive shall
first make oath that the person to whom the
labor or service of such fugitive is alleged
to be due is his lawful owner, and has not
borne arms against the United States in
the present rebellion, nor in any way given
aid and comfort thereto; and no person
engaged in the military or naval service of
the United States shall, under any pretence
whatever, assume to decide on the validity
of the claim of any person to the service or
labor of any other person, or surrender up
any such person to the claimant, on pain of
being dismissed from the service."

This nullified the fugitive slave laws. Escapees could not be returned to slavery if they escaped. This also applied to those who escaped to territories that had not yet achieved statehood.

And I do hereby enjoin upon and order all

persons engaged in the military and naval service of the United States to observe, obey, and enforce, within their respective spheres of service, the act, and sections above recited.

The military is commanded to enforce these provisions.

And the executive will in due time recommend that all citizens of the United States who shall have remained loyal thereto throughout the rebellion, shall (upon the restoration of the constitutional relation between the United States, and their respective States, and people, if that relation shall have been suspended or disturbed) be compensated for all losses by acts of the United States, including the loss of slaves.

Slaveholders in the Confederacy who remain loyal to the Union will be paid for their slaves.

In witness whereof, I have hereunto set my hand, and caused the seal of the United States to be affixed.

Done at the City of Washington this twenty-second day of September, in the year of our Lord, one thousand, eight hundred and sixty-two, and of the Independence of the United States the

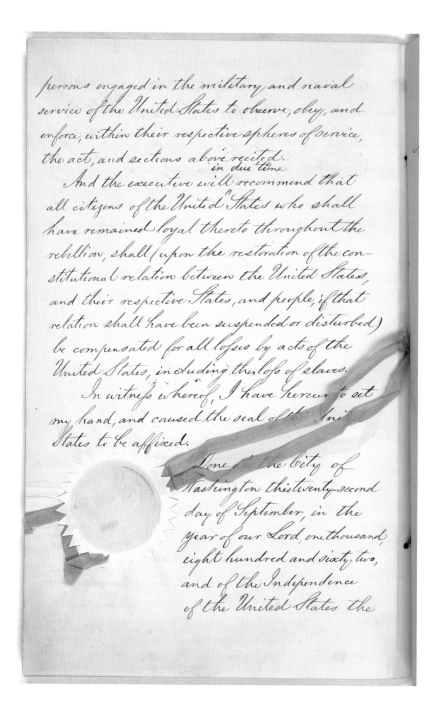

eighty seventh.

Abraham Lincoln

By the President:
William H. Seward,
Secretary of State

Reactions to the Preliminary Emancipation Proclamation ran the gamut from jubilant to contempt.

The Confederate States of America considered the Preliminary Emancipation Proclamation an order of a foreign power. They ignored it. Fierce fighting between Confederate and Union Army troops continued on battlefields throughout the South. [96]

Blacks like Frederick Douglass were displeased that the Preliminary Emancipation Proclamation "touched neither justice nor mercy." Some white abolitionists who had struggled on the side of freedom for decades like Lydia Maria Child chided that it was cold and "done reluctantly and stintedly."

Supremacist Democrats felt "the President has as much right to abolish the institution of marriage, or the laws of a State regulating the relation of parent and child, as to nullify the right of a State to regulate the relations of the white and black races." [97]

The Preliminary Emancipation Proclamation marked the last 100 days before which the institution of slavery would begin to be struck down, statute by statue, practice by practice.

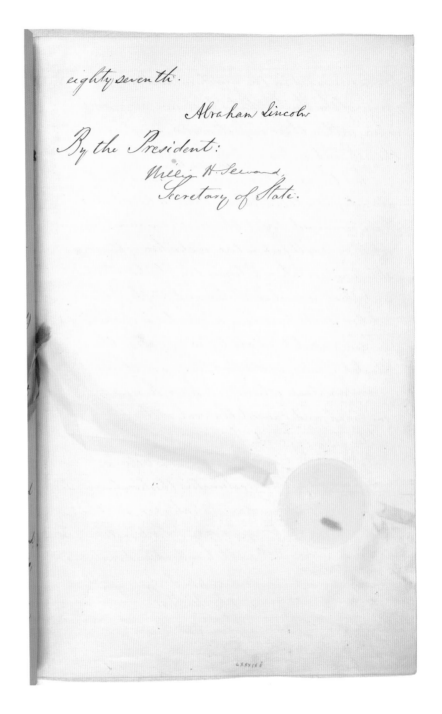

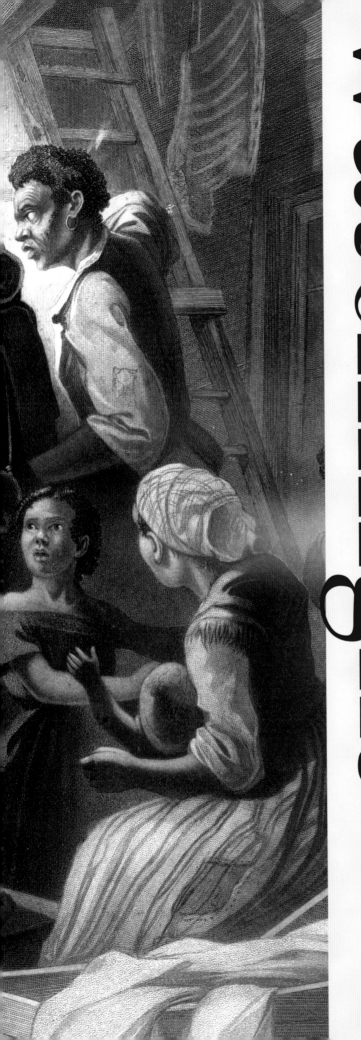

Watchnight

Anticipating a New Era

The diary of U.S. Navy Secretary Gideon Welles, a member of Abraham Lincoln's cabinet, revealed that when the President shared the Preliminary Emancipation Proclamation with his advisors, Lincoln told them that he had made a promise to God. "He had made a vow, a covenant" regarding "the cause of emancipation."[98]

The Bible had been one of the main texts used to justify slavery, with proponents pointing to scripture to support their view. The Quakers were the first Christian denomination to adopt a policy against slavery. But by the late 1700s a few British and American ministers adopted similar views and became some of the early abolitionists, using their Christian interpretations to denounce the slave trade and put an end to human bondage. However, most Christians continued to believe that there was a Biblical basis for slavery. They passed those beliefs on to generations that followed. Many slaveholders in the South were Christians, and some denominations, such as the Baptists split over this disagreement.[99]

Inspired by their religious beliefs, by the early 1800s white abolitionists began working with black abolitionists—many of whom were also religious leaders—to end to slavery. The

Steel engraving depicting an African American Union soldier reading the Emancipation Proclamation to an enslaved family. From the night of December 31st until the morning of January 1, 1863, many waited prayerfully for President Lincoln to sign the Emancipation Proclamation. That vigil became known as Watchnight—a commemoration continued today in African American churches.

Watchnight, the New Year's Eve worship service, is one of the most popular annual celebrations in African American churches—along with Easter, Christmas, and Mother's Day, one of the most attended services. Watchnight originated as enslaved and free African Americans, as well as abolitionists and other sympathetic whites, gathered in places of worship on New Year's Eve in anticipation of the promised signing of the Emancipation Proclamation by President Abraham Lincoln on January 1, 1863. Millions bring in the new year at watchnight services, such as the one pictured at St. Peter's A.M.E. Church in St.Louis, Missouri.

role of Northern Christians in the abolitionist movement was significant—from their secret acts of courage on behalf of fugitive slaves escaping through the Underground Railroad to widespread anti-slavery cultural influence of books like *Uncle Tom's Cabin*. (Harriet Beecher Stowe, who wrote *Uncle Tom's Cabin*, was a Congregationalist, and the daughter and sister of celebrated clergymen.) [100]

By the time of the Preliminary Emancipation Proclamation, black people in the North had long-established their own churches, which had cultivated black Christian leaders and also served as centers of their communities. Bethel African Methodist Episcopal Church in Philadelphia, for example, was established in 1794. African-American churches formed in the late 1700s still exist today. First African Baptist Church in Savannah, Georgia, the oldest existing black church in the U.S., was founded in 1788, just one year after the Constitution was adopted and before its ratification affirmed slavery as part of the founding document of the new nation. The Southern black church, pre-Emancipation, was the primary communal gathering place and often the base for liberation. The floorboards of the First African Baptist Church in Savannah still conceal hidden compartments used to help fugitive slaves or free blacks avoid re-enslavement. [101]

Although Africans from a variety of religious traditions were kidnapped or sold into slavery, once in the U.S., some Africans and many of their descendants eventually adopted the dominant white, Christian faith. Worship was regulated by the same separate, dehumanizing social strictures as other enslaved-black/free-white interactions. Some in bondage served slaveowners at church, and while there heard scriptures and sermons; some slaveholders took those they enslaved to worship in church. In other cases, slaveholders brought white ministers to plantations to preach to the enslaved, often emphasizing biblical references to slavery and obedience to authority.

Blacks, however, developed their own religious understanding. The Exodus story in the Bible, in which God delivered the Hebrews from slavery in Egypt resonated with those in bondage and became their story, highlighted by their own worship leaders. [102]

Given this history, the church was the natural place for African Americans and their allies to meet as the Preliminary Emancipation Proclamation brought the goal of freedom within view.

News of the Preliminary Emancipation Proclamation was quickly reported in the states and territories by telegraph and in newspapers the following day. Free blacks in the North and South would have had almost immedi-ate access to the news, but in remote Southern enslaved communities, many disrupted by the war, the news would have been spread by the black church.

Across the country, African-American churches began to plan worship services for December 31, 1862, with the express purpose of ushering in the New Year and the imminent arrival of Emancipation. These celebrations were called Freedom's Eve or "Watchnight" services, and are a continued tradition in black churches to this day. [103]

On December 23, 1862, a week before the cut-off date for Southern states to rejoin the Union on the 31st, Confederate president Jefferson Davis issued a response to the Preliminary Emancipation Proclamation. Davis's statement did not address Lincoln's offer to rejoin the Union. Instead, Davis threatened to treat free blacks as slaves if the Proclamation was enacted, since he recognized that the Preliminary Emancipation Proclamation could incite slaves to escape. He threatened to allow Con-

federates to re-enslave free blacks in the South, and even those in the North once their military was victorious.

As 1862 came to an end, the nation's African-descended population awaited the arrival of the New Year to see if the President would follow through with his ultimatum. Black churches became central in this time of heightened anticipation of emancipation.[104]

We can only imagine the drama of that first Watchnight. Free and enslaved worshipers gathered in churches as proud as Bethel African Methodist Episcopal Church in Philadelphia and First African Baptist Church in Savannah and as humble as outdoor campgrounds warmed only by campfires and quilts. On the evening of December 31, 1862, traditions that continue today began with songs, dramatic recitation of Scripture, prayers, clapping, testimony, wails, shouts and often tears in anticipation of the arrival of the New Year.

A stained glass window from the 16th Street Baptist Church in Birmingham, Alabama. In 1963, one hundred years after the Emancipation Proclamation, the church was bombed in an act of racist terrorism. Four little girls, attending Sunday School, were killed. Many cite this incident as the turning point that sparked a new wave of Civil Rights sentiment that mirrored abolitionism prior to emancipation.

From Selling Day to Freedom Day

Watchnight had an even deeper meaning for the enslaved, since it transformed what had been the worst time of the year into a day of hope.

During slavery, the last day of the year was selling day, when slave owners reconciled their books and often sold their human property to settle debts, often separating loved ones. Because so many slaves were sold at year's end, a family in bondage often dreaded New Year's Eve because it might be their last night together. Rather than waiting in fear to hear if their spouse or child or elderly parent would be sold—never to be seen again—the enslaved gathered in anticipation of hearing news of freedom.

These three slave narratives—autobiographies written or told by blacks who had once been enslaved—all mention "selling day" and the anguish felt on New Year's Eve before emancipation.

Incidents in the Life of a Slave Girl by **Harriet Jacobs** *(pen name Linda Brent)*

THE SLAVES' NEW YEAR'S DAY

Dr. Flint owned a fine residence in town, several farms, and about fifty slaves, besides hiring a number by the year. Hiring-day at the south takes place on the 1st of January. On the 2d, the slaves are expected to go to their new masters. On a farm, they work until the corn and cotton are laid. They then have two holidays. Some masters give them a good dinner under the trees. This over, they work until Christmas eve. If no heavy charges are meantime brought against them, they are given four or five holidays, whichever the master or overseer may think proper. Then comes New Year's eve; and they gather together their little alls, or more properly speaking, their little nothings, and wait anxiously for the dawning of day. At the appointed hour the grounds are thronged with men, women, and children, waiting, like criminals, to hear their doom pronounced. The slave is sure to know who is the most humane, or cruel master, within forty miles of him. It is easy to find out, on that day, who clothes and feeds his slaves well; for he is surrounded by a crowd, begging, "Please, massa, hire me this year. I will work very hard, massa." If a slave is unwilling to go with his new master, he is whipped, or locked up in jail, until he consents to go, and promises not

to run away during the year. Should he chance to change his mind, thinking it justifiable to violate an extorted promise, woe unto him if he is caught! The whip is used till the blood flows at his feet; and his stiffened limbs are put in chains, to be dragged in the field for days and days! …But to the slave mother New Year's day comes laden with peculiar sorrows. She sits on her cold cabin floor, watching the children who may all be torn from her the next morning; and often does she wish that she and they might die before the day dawns. She may be an ignorant creature, degraded by the system that has

brutalized her from childhood; but she has a mother's instincts, and is capable of feeling a mother's agonies. On one of these sale days, I saw a mother lead seven children to the auction-block. She knew that some of them would be taken from her; but they took all. The children were sold to a slave-trader, and their mother was bought by a man in her own town. Before night her children were all far away. She begged the trader to tell her where he intended to take them; this he refused to do. How could he, when he knew he would sell them, one by one, wherever he could command the highest price? I met that mother in the street, and her wild, haggard face lives to-day in my mind. She wrung her hands in anguish, and exclaimed, "Gone! all gone! Why don't God kill me?" I had no words wherewith to comfort her. Instances of this kind are of daily, yea, of hourly occurrence. Slaveholders have a method, peculiar to their institution, of getting rid of old slaves, whose lives have been worn out in their service. I knew an old woman, who for seventy years faithfully served her master. She had become almost helpless, from hard labor and disease. Her owners moved to Alabama, and the old black woman was left to be sold to anybody who would give twenty dollars for her.

Memories of Childhood's Slavery Days by Annie L. Burton

Leaves from a Slave's Journal of Life by Lewis Clarke

Separation of families? Yes, Indeed. If the gentleman had been in Kentucky at New Year's time, he wouldn't need to ask that question. Of all the days in the year, the slaves dread New-Year's day the worst of any. For folks come for their debts then; and if anybody is going to sell a slave, that's the time they do it; and if anybody's going to give away a slave, that's the time they do it; and the slave never knows where he'll be sent to. Oh, New-Year's a heart-breaking time in Kentucky!

© *Slave Testimony: Two Centuries of Letters, Speeches, Interviews, and Auto-biographies, Edited by John W. Blassin-game, LSU Press, 1977, Page 161*

The memory of my happy, care-free childhood days on the plantation, with my little white and black companions, is often with me. Neither master nor mistress nor neighbors had time to bestow a thought upon us, for the great Civil War was raging. That great event in American history was a matter wholly outside the realm of our childish interests. Of course we heard our elders discuss the various events of the great struggle, but it meant nothing to us.

On the plantation there were ten white children and fourteen colored children. Our days were spent roaming about from plantation to plantation, not knowing or caring what things were going on in the great world outside our little realm. Planting time and harvest time were happy days for us. How often at the harvest time the planters discovered cornstalks missing from the ends of the rows, and blamed the crows! We were called the "little fairy devils." To the sweet potatoes and peanuts and sugar cane we also helped ourselves.

Those slaves that were not married served the food from the great house, and about half-past eleven they would send the older children with food to the workers in the fields. Of course, I followed, and before we got to the fields, we had eaten the food nearly all up. When the workers returned home they complained, and we were whipped.

The slaves got their allowance every Monday night of molasses, meat, corn meal, and a kind of flour called "dredgings" or "shorts." Perhaps this allowance would be gone before the next Monday night, in which case the slaves would steal hogs and chickens. Then would come the whipping-post. Master himself never whipped his slaves; this was left to the overseer.

We children had no supper, and only a little piece of bread or something of the kind in the morning. Our dishes consisted of one wooden bowl, and oyster shells were our spoons. This bowl served for about fifteen children, and often the dogs and the ducks and the peafowl had a dip in it. Sometimes we had buttermilk and bread in our bowl, sometimes greens or bones.

Our clothes were little homespun cotton slips, with short sleeves. I never knew what shoes were until I got big enough to earn them myself.

If a slave man and woman wished to marry, a party would be arranged some Saturday night among the slaves. The marriage ceremony consisted of the pair jumping over a stick. If no children were born within a year or so, the wife was sold.

At New Year's, if there was any debt or mortgage on the plantation, the extra slaves were taken to Clayton and sold at the court house. In this way families were separated.

© *University of North Carolina at Chapel Hill.*

The Emancipation Proclamation

Many had expected Lincoln to sign the Emancipation Proclamation at the stroke of midnight on December 31st. But when he reviewed the draft copied by an assistant, he noticed a phrase that had been improperly transcribed. The Proclamation had to be rewritten.

Lincoln spent much of the morning of January 1, 1863, shaking hands with visitors as part of the traditional White House New Year's open house. According to his secretary, later, after the reception, as he reflected on the momentous occasion, Lincoln remarked:

I have been shaking hands since nine o'clock this morning and my right arm is almost paralyzed. If my name ever goes down in history it will be for this act, and my whole soul is in it. If my hand trembles when I sign the Proclamation all who examine the document hereafter will say 'He hesitated.'

He turned towards the table, took up the pen again and slowly, firmly signed his name, Abraham Lincoln, which the whole world now knows. Then he looked up, smiled, and said, "That will do." [105]

So, on the afternoon of January 1, 1863, his hand weary from greeting guests, Abraham Lincoln signed the Emancipation Proclamation.

January 1, 1863
A Transcription

(page 1)

By the President of the United States of America:
A Proclamation.

Whereas, on the twenty-second day of September, in the year of our Lord one thousand eight hundred and sixty-two, a proclamation was issued by the President of the United States, containing, among other things, the following, to wit:

"That on the first day of January, in the year of our Lord one thousand eight hundred and sixty-three, all persons held as slaves within any State or designated part of a State, the people whereof shall then be in rebellion against the United States, shall be then, thenceforward, and forever free; and the Executive Government of the United States, including the military and naval authority thereof, will recognize and maintain the freedom of such persons, and will do no act or acts to repress such persons, or any of them, in any efforts they may make for their actual freedom.

"That the Executive will, on the first day

By the President of the United States of America:

A Proclamation.

Whereas, on the twenty-second day of September, in the year of our Lord one thousand eight hundred and sixty-two, a proclamation was issued by the President of the United States, containing, among other things, the following, to wit:

"That on the first day of January, in the "year of our Lord one thousand eight hundred "and sixty-three, all persons held as slaves within "any State or designated part of a State, the people "whereof shall then be in rebellion against the "United States, shall be then, thenceforward, and "forever free; and the Executive Government of the "United States, including the military and naval "authority thereof, will recognize and maintain "the freedom of such persons, and will do no act "or acts to repress such persons, or any of them, "in any efforts they may make for their actual "freedom.

"That the Executive will, on the first day

... on the twenty-second day of September ... a proclamation was issued by the President ...

This section referred to the Preliminary Emancipation Proclamation and the next two paragraphs repeated what was in the Preliminary version.

... by virtue of the power in me vested as Commander-in-Chief, of the Army and Navy of the United States... as a fit and necessary war measure for suppressing said rebellion...

Because slavery was written into the Constitution, Lincoln used his wartime power as Commander-in-Chief to free the enslaved, but only in states and parts of states that were at war with the United States.

"of January aforesaid, by proclamation, designate "the States and parts of States, if any, in which the "people thereof, respectively, shall then be in rebellion "against the United States; and the fact that any "State, or the people thereof, shall on that day be, in "good faith, represented in the Congress of the United "States by members chosen thereto at elections "wherein a majority of the qualified voters of such "State shall have participated, shall, in the absence "of strong countervailing testimony, be deemed con‑ "clusive evidence that such State, and the people "thereof, are not then in rebellion against the "United States."

Now, therefore, I, Abraham Lincoln, President of the United States, by virtue of the power in me vested as Commander‑in‑ Chief, of the Army and Navy of the United States in time of actual armed rebellion against the authority and government of the United States, and as a fit and necessary war measure for sup‑ pressing said rebellion, do, on this first day of January, in the year of our Lord one thousand eight hundred and sixty‑three, and in accordance with my purpose so to do publicly proclaimed for the full period of one hundred days, from the day first above mentioned, order and designate as the States and parts of States wherein the people thereof respectively, are this day in rebellion against the United States, the following, to wit:

Arkansas, Texas, Louisiana, (except the Parishes of St. Bernard, Plaquemines, Jefferson, St. John, St. Charles, St. James Ascension, Assumption, Terrebonne, Lafourche, St. Mary, St. Martin, and Orleans, including the City of New Orleans) Mississippi, Alabama, Florida, Georgia, South Carolina, North Carolina, and Virginia, (except the forty-eight counties designated as West Virginia, and also the counties of Berkley, Accomac, Northampton, Elizabeth City, York, Princess Ann, and Norfolk, including the cities of Norfolk and Portsmouth, and which excepted parts are, for the present, left precisely as if this proclamation were not issued.

And by virtue of the power, and for the purpose aforesaid, I do order and declare that all persons held as slaves within said designated States, and parts of States, are, and henceforward shall be free; and that the Executive government of the United States, including the military, and naval authorities thereof, will recognize and maintain the freedom of said persons.

And I hereby enjoin upon the people so declared to be free to abstain from all violence; unless in necessary self-defence; and I recommend to them that, in all cases when allowed, they labor faithfully for reasonable wages.

And I further declare and make known, that such persons of suitable condition, will be received into the armed service of the United States to garrison forts, positions, stations, and other places, and to man vessels of all sorts in said service.

And upon this act, sincerely believed to be an act of justice, warranted by the Constitution, upon military necessity, I invoke the considerate judgment of mankind, and the gracious favor of Almighty God.

In witness whereof, I have hereunto set my hand and caused the seal of the United States to be affixed.

Done at the city of Washington, this first day of January, in the year of our Lord

(page 2)

of January aforesaid, by proclamation, designate the States and parts of States, if any, in which the people thereof, respectively, shall then be in rebellion against the United States; and the fact that any State, or the people thereof, shall on that day be, in good faith, represented in the Congress of the United States by members chosen thereto at elections wherein a majority of the qualified voters of such State shall have participated, shall, in the absence of strong countervailing testimony, be deemed conclusive evidence that such State, and the people thereof, are not then in rebellion against the United States."

Now, therefore I, Abraham Lincoln, President of the United States, by virtue of the power in me vested as Commander-in-Chief, of the Army and Navy of the United States in time of actual armed rebellion against the authority and government of the United States, and as a fit and necessary war measure for suppressing said rebellion, do, on this first day of January, in the year of our Lord one thousand eight hundred and sixty-three, and in accordance with my purpose so to do publicly proclaimed for the full period of one hundred days, from the

(page 3)

day first above mentioned, order and designate as the States and parts of States wherein the people thereof respectively, are this day in rebellion against the United States, the following, to wit:

Arkansas, Texas, Louisiana, (except the Parishes of St. Bernard, Plaquemines, Jefferson, St. John, St. Charles, St. James Ascension, Assumption, Terrebonne, Lafourche, St. Mary, St. Martin, and Orleans, including the City of New Orleans) Mississippi, Alabama, Florida, Georgia, South

Carolina, North Carolina, and Virginia, (except the forty-eight counties designated as West Virginia, and also the counties of Berkley, Accomac, Northampton, Elizabeth City, York, Princess Ann, and Norfolk, including the cities of Norfolk and Portsmouth[])], and which excepted parts, are for the present, left precisely as if this proclamation were not issued.

And by virtue of the power, and for the purpose aforesaid, I do order and declare that all persons held as slaves within said designated States, and parts of States, are, and henceforward shall be free; and that the Executive

(page 4)

government of the United States, including the military and naval authorities thereof, will recognize and maintain the freedom of said persons.

And I hereby enjoin upon the people so declared to be free to abstain from all violence, unless in necessary self-defence; and I recommend to them that, in all cases when allowed, they labor faithfully for reasonable wages.

And I further declare and make known, that such persons of suitable condition, will be received into the armed service of the United States to garrison forts, positions, stations, and other places, and to man vessels of all sorts in said service.

And upon this act, sincerely believed to be an act of justice, warranted by the Constitution, upon military necessity, I invoke the considerate judgment of mankind, and the gracious favor of Almighty God.

In witness whereof, I have hereunto set my hand and caused the seal of the United States to be affixed.

Done at the City of Washington, this first day of January, in the year of our Lord

(page 5)

one thousand eight hundred and sixty three, and of the Independence of the United States of America the eighty-seventh.

By the President: Abraham Lincoln
William H. Seward, Secretary of State.

Independence of the United States of America the eighty-seventh.

Since founded in 1776, the nation was eighty-seven years old when the institution of slavery was struck down by the Emancipation Proclamation.

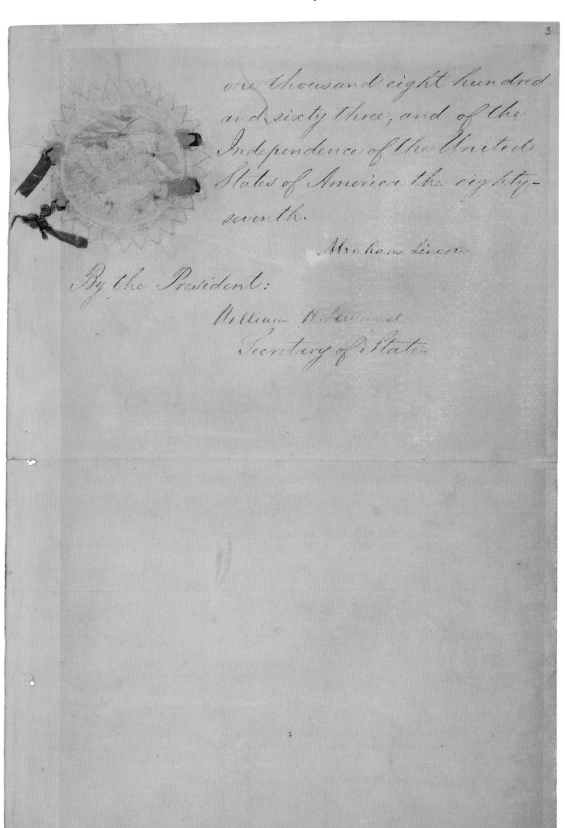

Reverend Henry McNeal Turner brought news of the Emancipation Proclamation to worshipers at Washington's Israel Bethel AME Church, and its reading prompted enthusiastic celebration. Turner described the excitement, but he was so winded from running to the church with a copy of the document that was printed in the newspaper, that he could not catch his breath to read it. Someone else read it to the congregants. (Washington's Israel Bethel AME Church is now the site of the Rayburn House Office Building on Capitol Hill.)

"Seeing such a multitude of people in and around the church," the pastor, Henry McNeal Turner, said, "I hurriedly went up to the office of the first paper in which the proclamation of freedom could be printed, known as the 'Evening Star,' and squeezed myself through the dense crowd that was wait-

ing for the paper. The first sheet run off with the proclamation in it was grabbed for by three of us, but some active young man got possession of it and fled. The next sheet was grabbed for by several, and was torn into tatters.

The third sheet from the press was grabbed for by several, but I succeeded in procuring so much of it as contained the proclamation, and off I went for life and death. Down Pennsylvania I ran as for my

life, and when the people saw me coming with the paper in my hand raised a shouting cheer that was almost deafening. As many as could get around me lifted me to a great platform, and I started to read the proclamation. I had run the best end of a mile, I was out of breath, and could not read. Mr. Hinton to whom I handed the paper, read it with great force and clearness. While he was reading every kind of demonstration and gesticulation was going on.

Men squealed, women fainted, dogs barked, white and colored people shook hands, songs were sung, and by this time cannons began to fire at the navy-yard, and follow in the wake of the roar that had for some time been going on behind the White House...It was indeed a time of times, and a half time, nothing like it will ever be seen again in this life." [106]

War after the Proclamation and the End of Slavery

Although Confederate leaders and southerners in general ignored the Emancipation Proclamation, many enslaved African Americans seized freedom. A second wave of former slaves set off from plantations, amid the fighting of the Civil War. Although freed by the Emancipation Proclamation, enslaved blacks in the Confederate states were not able to realize their freedom "forever" until the North had won the war.

For African-American men who left slavery behind, the Proclamation provided an opportunity to enlist in the Union Army. Northern states had refused to enlist black volunteers before the Proclamation. But even after it was signed, and although it expressly provided for black enlistment, many northern states were still reluctant to enlist black soldiers. Eventually 180,000 African Americans joined the Union Army providing momentum to the Union Army's efforts to end the war.

Because Lincoln maintained the Emancipation Proclamation was a wartime measure,[108] those enslaved whom it had deemed "forever free," needed to be assured liberation during peace time. That was to be accomplished by an amendment to the document, which from the nation's founding had affirmed slavery—the U.S. Constitution.

The Thirteenth Amendment to the United States Constitution officially outlawed slavery and involuntary servitude, except as punishment for a crime. With a 38-to-6 vote, the U.S. Senate passed the Thirteenth Amendment on April 8, 1864, more than a year after Lincoln's Emancipation Proclamation and while the Civil War still raged. The House of Representatives passed the Thirteenth Amendment more

Private Hubbard Pryor, formerly enslaved, is shown before and after donning the Union Soldier Blue. More than 200,000 black men fought in the Union Army or Navy. Despite low pay, inadequate training, and brutal treatment if captured, black soldiers stood the test, proving their skill and bravery. For valor displayed in battle, eighteen African American soldiers and seven African American sailors were awarded the Congressional Medal of Honor. Wrote Frederick Douglass, "Let the black man get upon his person the brass letter, U.S., let him get an eagle on his button, and a musket on his shoulder and bullets in his pocket, there is no power on [E]arth that can deny that he has earned the right to citizenship." Lincoln proclaimed, "Without the military help of the black freedmen, the war against the South could not have been won."

than two years after the Emancipation Proclamation, on January 31, 1865, by a 119-to 56 vote, with eight abstentions. The congressional votes ultimately confirmed that the Civil War, if won by Union forces, would likely result in freedom for those bound by slavery. But amendments to the Constitution require ratification by three fourths of the state legislatures. Two years after the Emancipation Proclamation, the Thirteenth Amendment was being debated in the legislatures of Union states, even as the bloody Civil War dragged on. [109]

In January 1865, Field Order No. 15 was issued by General William T. Sherman distributing land that had been abandoned by plantation owners to freedmen who had remained in the areas, as the Union troops took control of Confederate regions along the coast. The land was distributed in forty acre plots, and a government mule was loaned to freedmen. This is the source of the phrase "40 acres and a mule." [110]

By the spring of 1865, the tides of the war had clearly shifted in favor of the Union Army. In early April, the Union army in Virginia had the Confederate forces on the run and gained control of Richmond, the capital of the Confederacy. Confederate legislators fled Richmond in advance of the Union troops. On April 9, 1865, General Robert E. Lee, commander of the Confederate troops surrendered to General Ulysses S. Grant, commander of the Union Army. The rebellion and secession by the Confederate States of America had been defeated and those southern states could no longer consider the Emancipation Proclamation an order issued by a foreign power. Permanent changes to the U. S. Constitution, outlawing slavery, were being ratified by state assemblies.

Five days after Lee's surrender, the "Great Emancipator" President Abraham Lincoln was assassinated. [111]

His successor, former U.S. Vice President Andrew Johnson, proved to be an obstacle to African Americans'

The 29th Connecticut Infantry Regiment (Colored) at camp at Beaufort South Carolina. The 29th was organized for enlisted men near Fair Haven, Connecticut, from December 1863 to March 1864. In April, it was ordered to Hilton Head, SC, and performed guard duty in Beaufort. It holds the honor of being the first regiment to enter Richmond on April 3, 1865, the day after General Robert E. Lee evacuated the capital, ending nine months under siege. The Fall of Richmond is considered the beginning of the end of the Civil War.

realization of life, liberty and pursuit of happiness through economic and social independence. By September of 1865, Johnson demanded that Field Order No. 15 landowners, who were living on the lands and approaching their first harvest on farms along the southeastern coast, return the land to the former owners. He did not want to establish a policy of giving away property without compensation to the former owners, even though those landowners had fought against the United States. He wanted the former slaveowners to reclaim their land.[112]

Still, the Thirteenth Amendment, abolishing slavery, was successfully ratified by the required number of state legislatures and was adopted on December 18, 1865. The Thirteenth Amendment to the Constitution legally ended slavery in the U.S.[113]

The Fourteenth Amendment,

This unidentified Black soldier in uniform poses with his wife and twin daughters. Families were proud of their soldier husbands and fathers, despite facing financial hardship and ill treatment from angry slaveholders when black men fought in the Civil War.

which provided that anyone born in the United States was a citizen and as such would be entitled to all the rights of citizenship, was ratified in 1868. This amendment overturned the Supreme Court Dred Scott decision of 1857, which excluded blacks—both enslaved and free—from citizenship. The Fifteenth Amendment, ratified in 1870, granted (men only) voting rights regardless of "race, color, or previous condition of servitude."[114]

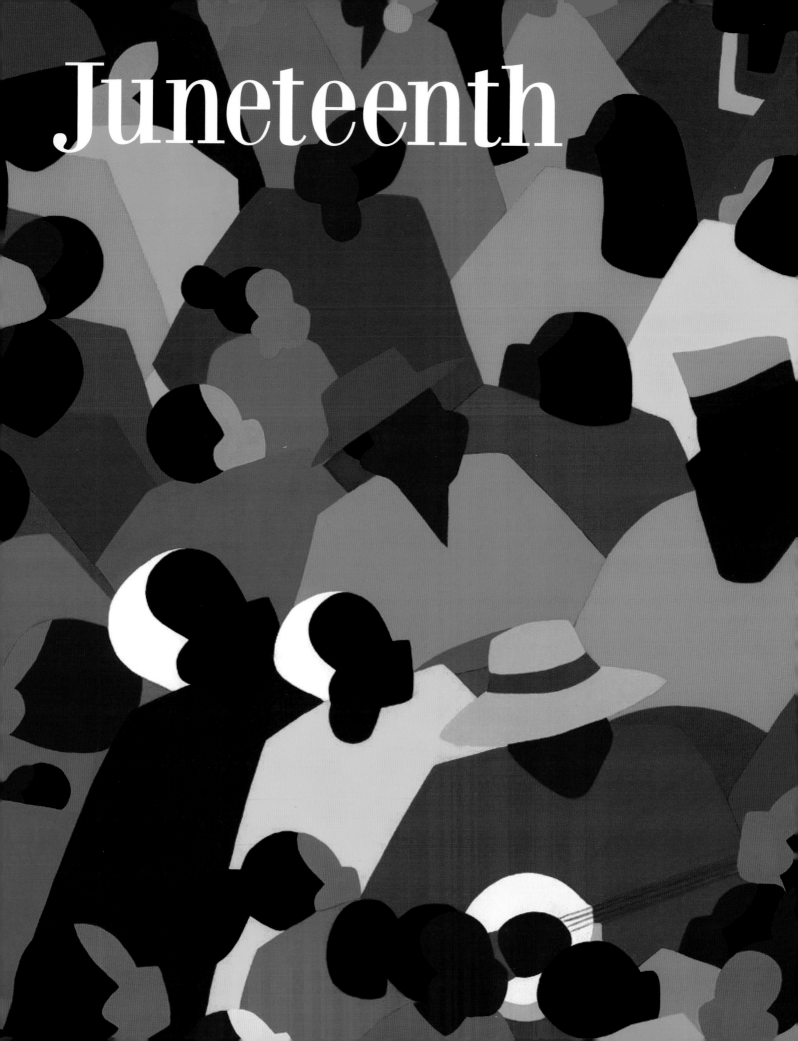

Juneteenth

And Other Emancipation Day Celebrations

Although some held in bondage fled to freedom upon hearing the news of the Emancipation Proclamation, most remained enslaved. The perspective of white residents of the Confederacy was the Proclamation had no authority over them. And in most cases, the enslaved were only freed when Union Army troops gained control of Confederate territory, which progressed with each Union victory from the signing of the Proclamation until the end of the war. Even after the war had officially ended, some slaveholders still refused to free the enslaved. Fighting continued after Lee's surrender to Grant, which formally ended the Civil War. Only after the arrival of Union troops to specific areas of Confederate resistance did slaveholders reluctantly free those who had been enslaved. There were countless examples of how news of Emancipation spread throughout the South.

On June 19, 1865, more than two months after Lee's surrender, Union soldiers led by Major General Gordon Granger arrived

Acrylic painting by Dr. Synthia Saint James capturing the festivities and uniting atmosphere of Juneteenth, the day Union soldiers arrived in Galveston, Texas, with the news that the Civil War had ended and the enslaved were free. Today Juneteenth is celebrated in communities across the nation and marks African American freedom and achievement.

at Galveston, Texas and issued General Order Number 3, which began:

"The people of Texas are informed that in accordance with a Proclamation from the Executive of the United States, all slaves are free. This involves an absolute equality of rights and rights of property between former masters and slaves, and the connection heretofore existing between them becomes that between employer and free laborer…"

This information had been withheld from the enslaved, even after the war had formally ended.

Freedom for the enslaved in Galveston, Texas, was considered the final act of emancipation associated with the Proclamation. In Galveston in 1865, African Americans celebrated the news of freedom, calling the celebration "Juneteenth" to honor the date, June nineteenth.

Finally on April 2, 1866, Abraham Lincoln's successor formally declared the Civil War was over:

"Now, therefore, I, Andrew Johnson, President of the United States, do hereby proclaim and declare that the insurrection which heretofore existed in the States of Georgia, South Carolina, Virginia, North Carolina, Tennessee, Alabama, Louisiana, Arkansas, *Mississippi, and Florida, is at an end and is henceforth to be so regarded."*

Since Texas was not mentioned in his initial statement, Johnson issued a new proclamation on August 20, 1866, after the Texas state government was formed:

"I do further proclaim that the said insurrection is at an end and that peace, order, tranquility, and civil authority now exists in and throughout the whole of the United States of America."

In Texas, Juneteenth celebrations continued annually and spread among African Americans to other parts of the country in recognition that actual emancipation came many months after the Emancipation Proclamation.

Florida observes emancipation in an unofficial commemoration on May 20th, when Union Army Major-General Edward McCook announced freedom of the enslaved in a speech in Tallahassee, in which he gave the first reading of the Emancipation Proclamation in Florida on May 20, 1865.

Washington, D.C. celebrates emancipation on April 16, the day in 1862—eight months before the Emancipation Proclamation was announced—President Lincoln signed the Compensated Emancipation Act, in which the federal government compensated slave holders, and released every slave in the District of Columbia. [116]

Mississippi celebrates an emancipation day on May 8, known as "Eight o' May," the date a month after Lee's surrender in 1865, when Confederate troops still holding out in Mississippi, Alabama and east Louisiana were "paroled"—a military term meaning they would no longer fight. [117]

Kentucky celebrates Emancipation Day on August 8, the anniversary of the day the enslaved in Paducah and McCracken counties learned of their freedom.

Juneteenth celebrations were important affirmations of actual liberation dates experienced in various states, and were part of African-American culture for decades after the Emancipation Proclamation. In the first half of the twentieth century, such

observances declined. The Civil Rights movement of the 1950s and 1960s led to a revival in Emancipation celebrations.

Music helped sustain those in bondage under what many historians assert was the most dehumanizing form of slavery ever practiced. More than 400 songs from the pre-Emancipation period have been documented and preserved. Many of them, like this one that is still sung in churches today, reflect on freedom:

Jesus, I'll never forget
what you done for me
Jesus, I'll never forget
that you set me free
Jesus, I'll never forget
how you brought me out
no I'll never forget
No never

Opposite page: Emancipation Day 1866 in Washington, D.C.

Left: Juneteenth celebrations—like this one at Sabayet, Inc., a community outreach center in St. Louis, Missouri— are still immensely popular in many Black communities. On January 1, 1980, Texas was the first state to recognize Juneteenth as an official state holiday.

A New
Fight for Freedom
Begins

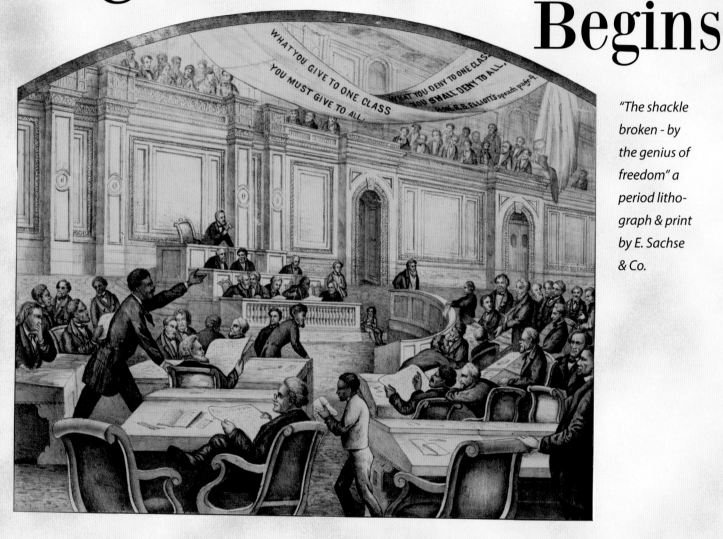

"The shackle broken - by the genius of freedom" a period lithograph & print by E. Sachse & Co.

Immediately after the end of the Civil War, African-American freedmen and women sought to reunite with family members who they had been separated from during slavery. Children and parents, who had been sold away from one another during slavery, went on long, often lonely searches to find each other. Wedding ceremonies were among the most numerous and socially significant outcomes of this new-found freedom, as formerly enslaved husbands and wives, who did not have the legal status to marry, sought to declare their lifelong commitments.

Although the Emancipation Proclamation and the Thirteenth Amendment ended slavery in the United States, and allowed blacks to begin to build deep human connections, which slavery had denied them, the four million African Americans, who were "forever free," faced tremendous challenges in creating new lives for themselves. How would they support themselves? Where would they live? What rights did they have to go to certain places? To vote? To hold political office? The country was accustomed to seeing blacks as enslaved. And many whites, even those who believed slavery as wrong, thought the conditions and behavior of the newly freed was due to racial inferiority rather than the deprivations of slavery.[118]

Official obstacles like President Andrew Johnson's reversal of the "40 acres and a mule" land transfer, were compounded by social barriers as well, in the form of racially motivated violence and intimidation by individuals and groups of white men who targeted African Americans on the roads, in schools, in churches, and in their homes. In 1866, the Ku Klux Klan was formed as a secret organization whose white-hooded night riders traveled on horseback attacking blacks and their white allies who the Klan decided were challenging the southern system of racial oppression.[119]

At a time when wage labor was not common in the South, blacks sought to construct lives as independent farmers, attempting to acquire land for farming, either through purchase or through the Southern Homestead Act of 1866, which made government land in Arkansas, Alabama, Florida, Kentucky and Mississippi available for free or at minimal cost as long as it was farmed. There were tremendous challenges both economically and socially in acquiring land. But some African Americans were successful. In **Black Reconstruction** W.E.B. Du Bois noted: *"Virginia Negroes acquired between 80,000 and 100,000 acres of land during the late sixties and early seventies. There were soon a few prosperous Negro farms with 400 to 1,000 acres*

1863 Emancipation Proclamation goes into effect freeing slaves in states in and areas in rebellion.

1863 Massachusetts 54th Regiment is first all-black regiment raised in the free states.

1865 The Thirteenth Amendment is ratified, prohibiting slavery and involuntary servitude in the U.S., except as punishment for a crime. President Lincoln assassinated. Black Codes written by state legislatures to require separation of races in public places and facilities. Increasingly restrictive, Black Codes affect work, contracts and free movement, creating quasi slavery.

▲ Bureau of Refugees, Freedmen and Abandoned Lands (Freedmen's Bureau) established.

Enslaved African Americans in Texas learn they are free, create celebration of Juneteenth.

1866 Civil Rights Act of 1866 passed, conferring citizenship upon black Americans and guaranteeing freedmen equal rights with whites to make and enforce contracts and to purchase, sell or lease property.

1867 Reconstruction Acts passed, enfranchises black men in the South.

of land and some owners of considerable city property. Georgia Negroes had bought, by 1875, 396,658 acres of land assessed at $1,263,902…"[120]

The Freedmen's Bureau, a federal government agency created in 1865 to assist formerly enslaved blacks with the transition to freedom, never had the clout required to help many overcome the obstacles of economic and racial prejudice.[121]

Soon, most Southern states enacted Black Codes, laws that restricted the movement of African Americans, and required them to enter into labor contracts (for meager wages) to work on farms under the threat of arrest. When they were arrested they could be "leased" to work on white-owned farms. The codes were a daunting restriction on African Americans' freedom.[122]

As the obstacles against African Americans increased, supported implicitly by President Johnson's racial hostility, his fellow Republicans became increasingly frustrated with his intransigence in including African Americans in the rebuilding of the South. In 1867, over Johnson's veto, Congress passed the Reconstruction Act, which required that the South to be divided into five military districts, each with a federally appointed governor, and with federal troops stationed in the South to enforce laws that required states to write new constitutions that included the right for black men to vote. In many of these states, African Americans were a substantial portion of the population. This was the beginning of Radical Reconstruction.[123]

During Radical Reconstruction—from 1867 to 1877—African Americans in the South tasted freedom for the first time. With federal government support, African Americans Hiram Revels and Blanche Bruce were elected to the U.S. Senate representing Mississippi. P.B.S. Pinchback was appointed governor of Louisiana. More than fifteen African-American men were elected to Congress. More than 1500 hundred African Americans served in public office in the South at the state, local and national levels during Reconstruction. Public school systems were established in southern states for the first time, and although most were segregated, they provided African-American children and adults with the first opportunity to obtain an education. Historically black colleges and universities—including Hampton, Fisk and Morehouse colleges among others—were founded during this period. Many also had high schools that were affiliated with these colleges.

For many white southerners, freedom for African Americans was offensive to the "southern way of life." By the early 1870s, white hostility towards black freedom resulted in violent attacks on African-American elected officials, churches, entrepreneurs, teachers and their white allies to "redeem"—or regain—control of the South. At the same time, Northerners, who were experiencing economic problems of their own, grew tired of supporting the Reconstruction effort. They were convinced by Southerner whites that they understood

94

1868 Congress ratifies Fourteenth Amendment, defining citizens as those born or naturalized, including former slaves. Any state that denied or abridged voting rights of males over 21 would be subject to proportional reductions in its representation in the U.S. House of Representatives.

John W. Menard (LA) first African American elected to Congress. Neither he nor his opponent is seated due to election results dispute; Oscar Dunn (LA) elected first black lieutenant governor in the U.S.

1870 Colored Methodist Episcopal Church organized. Known today as the Christian Methodist Episcopal Church.

Fifteenth Amendment ratified, declaring "right of citizens of the U.S. to vote shall not be denied or abridged by the U.S. or by any state on account of race, color, or previous condition of servitude."

Joseph Rainey (SC) first African American elected to the U.S. House of Representatives.

▲ Hiram Revels (MS) first African American elected and seated in the Senate, serving one year and completing the term of former President of the Confederacy Jefferson Davis.

how to deal with "their" black population.

Reconstruction played a role in the presidential election of 1876, which resulted in a deadlock between the anti-slavery, Republican Party candidate Rutherford B. Hayes and Democrat Samuel B. Tilden. Negotiations led to a compromise in which Hayes took office in 1877 in exchange for agreeing not to enforce Reconstruction laws. Reconstruction was over.[124]

The following decades saw a rollback of African American progress in the South. Through intimidation and voter fraud, Redemption Democrats gained control of southern states. By the 1880s and 1890s, Southern states had enacted laws requiring racial segregation in public places—in what were called Jim Crow laws—relegating African Americans to second-class citizenship. Lynching and other acts of violence against blacks and their property increased, (usually hangings) as well as accusations of crimes—but without legal charges—were increasing, with black men as the primary targets. Often such false accusations of criminality were sparked by jealousy over black economic success, or a failure to be appropriately deferential or submissive to whites. Historian Rayford Logan called the period "the nadir," or low point of race relations in America.[125]

Yet many, like Ida B. Wells and W.E.B. Du Bois, continued to agitate for full rights for black people. The formation of the National Association for the Advancement of Colored People (NAACP) in 1909, and the National Urban League in 1910, established organizations to help mount legal challenges, protests and other initiatives for African Americans. A. Philip Randolph joined the ranks of these activists, first as editor of *The Messenger* magazine in the 1910s, and beginning in the 1920s as the leader of the Brotherhood of Sleeping Car Porters, the largest black union in the country. They and many others laid the groundwork for the modern-day freedom or Civil Rights Movement. [126]

Milestones in the first 100 years of Post-Emancipation freedom efforts

1867 Radical Reconstruction begins

1868 The 14th Amendment is ratified

1870 The 15th Amendment is ratified

1875 The Civil Rights Act is passed

1896 Homer Plessy challenges Louisiana segregation laws; Plessy v Ferguson Supreme Court decision affirms constitutionality of racial segregation

1905 The Niagara Movement civil rights organization founded

1909 NAACP formed

1910 National Urban League formed

1917 Silent Protest march (New York City) rallies against the race riots in East St. Louis, Illinois, in which whites attacked and killed 48 African Americans, injured hundreds and burned their homes to the ground. This was only one of many similar Northern riots in the first two decades of the 1900s where whites committed violent acts against African Americans. Typically such riots were sparked by increased racial

▼ Between 1870 and 1877, the period of Radical Reconstruction, 16 black men served in Congress.

American Anti-Slavery Society disbands, believing it accomplished its goals.

1871 Fisk Jubilee Singers tour America and Europe to raise funds for their college.

P.B.S. Pinchback (LA) elected president pro tem and acting lieutenant governor upon death of Oscar Dunn.

1872 Pinchback sworn in as Governor of Louisiana to complete term of impeached governor. He was in office for 35 days, serving out the term.

1874 Charles Summer, esteemed white advocate of rights for African Americans dies.

1875 Congress passes Civil Rights Act, giving blacks equal rights on public accommodations and the right to serve on juries. Supreme Court would rule it invalid in 1883.

Blanche K. Bruce (MS) first African American elected to serve a full term in the U.S. Senate.

James A. Healy first African-American Roman Catholic priest and first African-American Roman Catholic bishop in the U.S.

tensions as large numbers of African Americans migrated from the South or rural areas and their increased numbers often led to tension over jobs. African Americans were discriminated against in factory jobs, and because they were desperate for work, factory owners often hired them as temporary replacement workers during union strikes by white workers.

The Red Summer of 1919 saw the most violent series of white-on-black race riots in the first half of the 20th century, with such riots continuing later in Tulsa (1921) and Rosewood, FL (1923). The impetus was white anger over black economic success.

1918 The "Harlem Hellfighters" soldiers awarded the Croix de Guerre by the French to the black soldiers who fought valiantly in World War I, although denied their citizenship rights at home.

1920s Harlem Renaissance brings visibility to African-American artists

1935 Works Progress Administration (WPA) provides jobs for African Americans during the Great Depression

1941 President Franklin Roosevelt signs Executive Order 8802, outlawing discrimination in war industry factories, in response to A. Phillip Randolph's threat to organize a March on Washington

1948 Harry Truman signs Executive Order 9981, desegregating the armed forces

1954 Brown vs. Board of Education Supreme Court decision outlaws discrimination in public education

1955 Montgomery bus boycott begins

1876 Supreme Court rules 15th Amendment does not guarantee black suffrage; only allows for punishment for denying vote based on race, color or previous condition of servitude.

1877 In "Compromise of 1877," Republican Rutherford B. Hayes becomes president and the last federal troops withdraw from the South, effectively ending Reconstruction.

1879 30,000 Blacks weary of discrimination, join Exoduster Movement leaving the South for North and West.

1880 Baptist Foreign Mission Convention convenes in Montgomery, AL; forerunner to the National Baptist Convention, USA.

1881 Tennessee passes first Jim Crow laws.

1882 Tuskegee Institute (Tuskegee University) and Chicago Tribune begin keeping records of lynchings in America. Recorded lynchings total 113, with 64 white and 49 black victims.

1883 Civil Rights Act overturned — Federal Government cannot bar corporations or individuals from discriminating on the basis of race.

1884 Moses Fleetwood Walker, catcher with a Toledo team, first black major league player.

1885 Cuban Giants organized by Frank P. Thompson, first group of professional black baseball players.

1888 First two Black-owned banks — Savings Bank of the Grand Fountain United Order of the Reformers, in Richmond, VA, and Capital Savings Bank of Washington D.C.—open their doors.

1892 Activist Ida B. Wells begins anti-lynching campaign with the publication of *Southern Horrors: Lynch Law in All Its Phases*.

Recorded lynchings number 161 blacks and 69 whites. According to the Tuskegee University archives, this would be the highest recorded number of African Americans and highest total recorded lynchings between1882 and1968.

1895 At Cotton States Exposition in Atlanta, black leader and educator Booker T. Washington expresses race relations can best be solved gradually through black self reliance and friendly relationship with whites.

1896 Plessy v. Ferguson established separate but equal public facilities.

National Association of Colored Women established in Wash. D.C. It will sponsor social and educational programs.

1897 The Church of God in Christ is formed. It will become the fifth largest Christian Church in America.

1898 National Afro American Council formed, widely considered the first national civil rights organization in the United States.

George H. White (NC) elected to his second (1898-1901) and final term as U.S. Congressman. With the rise of Jim Crow and repression of rights of African Americans, White would be the last black congressman of the post-Reconstruction era.

1900 National Negro Business League organized, Booker T. Washington named president. James Weldon Johnson and J. Rosamond Johnson compose "Lift Ev'ry Voice and Sing."

1903 *Souls of Black Folk* published by intellectual and activist W.E.B. Du Bois. It opposes Washington's gradual acceptance by whites and promotes black agitation for full civil rights.

▲ **1905** Niagara Movement established by group led by Du Bois and William Monroe Trotter.

1907 Madame C.J. Walker of Denver creates one of the most successful hair and cosmetics firms in the nation. She is regarded as the nation's first self made female millionaire.

1909 National Association for the Advancement of Colored People (NAACP) established on 100th anniversary of Lincoln's birth.

1910 NAACP publishes *Crisis Magazine*, edited by Du Bois. The first two issues have a militant tone opposing discrimination and segregation.

1911 Groundwork laid for National Urban League to assist Southern Blacks migrating to the North; The Great Migration of African Americans begins in 1915.

1913 African Americans celebrate the 50th anniversary of the Emancipation Proclamation with major celebrations in Jackson, MS, New Orleans, and Nashville.

1915 Association for the Study of Negro Life and History (today the Association for the Study of African American Life and History) founded as a major center on black history and thought.

1916 Jamaican Marcus Garvey establishes the New York division of the Universal Negro Improvement Association to build political, social and economic power among the African Diaspora.

1917 The United States enters World War I. Some 370,000 African-Americans join the segregated armed forces.

Ten thousand blacks march down New York's Fifth Avenue in silent parade protesting lynching.

1919 The Associated Negro Press is established in Chicago by Claude A. Barnett.

Race riots of whites attacking blacks erupt in 26 cities during the "Red Summer of 1919."

1920 Beginning of the Harlem Renaissance, a period of remarkable creativity by black artists and acceptance by white audiences. Rube Foster organizes National Negro Baseball League. Legendary league players include Satchel Paige, pitcher, and Josh Gibson, hitter. African Americans have played professional ball since 1884.

1921 Dyer Anti-Lynching Bill that would make lynching a federal crime introduced in Congress. The bill would be defeated three times.

1923 The National Urban League begins publishing *Opportunity: A Journal of Negro Life*. It becomes a forum for artists and authors of the Harlem Renaissance.

1925 International Brotherhood of Sleeping Car Porters and Maids organized. Asa Philip Randolph is chosen president.

The National Bar Association, an organization of black attorneys, established.

1926 Historian Carter G. Woodson establishes first Negro History Week, later to become Black History Month.

1928 Oscar DePriest elected to U.S. Congress, first black Congressman from the North and first since 1901

1931 Nine boys from Scottsboro, AL. arrested– falsely accused of raping two white women. Convicted on hearsay, the trial outcome roused national and international protest.

1934 Percentage of population on relief during the Great Depression is 52% among African Americans in urban northern cities compared to 13% among whites; 38% among African Americans in the south compared to 11% among whites.

1935 National Council of Negro Women established. Mary McLeod Bethune elected president. In 1936, she is chosen as director of Negro Affairs of the National Youth Administration—first significant federal appointment of an African American woman.

1938 Missouri ex rel. Gaines v. Canada rules that a state must provide equal educational facilities for African Americans. Gaines, the plaintiff, disappeared after the decision, never located.

1939 Jane M. Bolin first African American woman judge in the U.S. when appointed to the domestic relations court of New York City.

▲ Contralto Marian Anderson performs on the steps of the Lincoln Memorial for 75,000 after the Daughters of the American Revolution (DAR) refused to let her sing at their Constitution Hall. First Lady Eleanor Roosevelt and others resigned from the DAR in protest.

1940 Richard Wright publishes *Native Son*. It becomes an immediate best-seller, selling 250,000 hardcover copies within three weeks of its publication by the Book-of-the-Month Club.

Benjamin Oliver Davis, Sr. named first black general in the U.S. Army.

1941 Asa Phillip Randolph calls for 100,000 African Americans to march on Washington, D.C. to protest discrimination in armed forces. President Roosevelt issues Executive Order 8802, banning federal discrimination. The march is called off.

U. S. declares war on Japan with bombing of Pearl Harbor. African Americans institute Double V Campaign: Victory over fascism abroad, and discrimination at home. More than 2.5 million black men registered for the draft; more than one million had served in the war.

Charles Drew, M.D., establishes pioneer blood bank at NY Presbyterian Hospital. It is a prototype for donor banks used to collect blood for U.S. Armed Forces.

1942 Congress of Racial Equality (CORE), a nonviolent protest group, founded by James Farmer and students at University of Chicago.

First black cadets graduate from the Army Flight School at Tuskegee Institute, AL.

1944 Smith v. Allwright rules that white primaries are unconstitutional.

1945 United Nations founded in San Francisco, W.E.B. Du Bois, Mary McLeod Bethune, Ralph Bunche and Walter White in attendance.

John H. Johnson publishes first issue of Ebony magazine.

1946 Morgan v. Virginia rules that segregation in interstate bus travel is unconstitutional.

President Harry Truman creates Committee on Civil Rights to study federal policies and practices.

1947 CORE and Fellowship of Reconciliation send first bus of black and white Freedom Riders through South to test compliance with ban on segregating interstate buses.

▶ Jackie Robinson signs baseball contract with Brooklyn Dodgers, becoming the first African American to play for the major league club.

John Hope Franklin's *From Slavery to Freedom* is published. It will become the most popular textbook on African American history published in the 20th Century.

1948 Executive Order 9981 ends segregation and discrimination in the armed forces and federal employment.

U.S. Supreme Court rules in Shelley v. Kraemer that state and local governments cannot uphold segregation in housing covenants.

1950 Landmark Supreme Court case Sweatt v. Painter successfully challenges separate but equal established by Plessy v. Ferguson.

Henderson v. the United States rules dining cars on interstate trains cannot be segregated.

Ralph Bunche first African American to receive Nobel Peace Prize for mediation of Palestine conflict.

Gwendolyn Brooks wins a Pulitzer Prize, for her book *Annie Allen*.

1951 Florida NAACP pioneers Harry T. and Harriette Moore killed by a bombing of their home—first murder of prominent Civil Rights leaders.

1952 Ralph Ellison pens *Invisible Man*, winner of a National Book Award.

1953 Baton Rouge citizens stage first bus boycott of the Civil Rights movement.

Malcolm X named assistant minister of the Nation of Islam's (NOI) Temple Number One in Detroit. He would emerge as one of the most influential members of the NOI, second only to the Honorable Elijah Muhammad.

1954 Landmark Brown v. Board of Education of Topeka rules that "separate but equal" educational facilities are inherently unequal and therefore unconstitutional.

1955 Montgomery Bus Boycott organized when Rosa Parks refuses to give up her seat. Martin Luther King, Jr., elected president of the boycott operation.

Fourteen-year-old Emmett Till of Chicago murdered in Moody, MS. The sight of his brutalized body in his open casket pushed many on the sidelines into the Civil Rights Movement.

1956 After six-month boycott, buses in Tallahassee, FL, are desegregated; Montgomery Bus Boycott ends in victory for African Americans.

University of Alabama admits first African American student. She is expelled six months later for making "false and outrageous" statements about the university.

Executive Order 10590 creates the President's Committee on Government Policy to enforce policy of nondiscrimination in federal employment.

1957 Civil Rights Act of 1957 creates Commission on Civil Rights and establishes the Civil Rights Division in the U.S. Department of Justice. It authorizes Attorney General to seek court injunctions against obstruction of rights by state officials.

Black ministers form the Southern Christian Leadership Conference.

President Dwight D. Eisenhower orders federal troops to protect black students entering Central High School in Little Rock, Ark.

1958 Louis E. Lomax, hired by WNTA-TV in New York City, first African American newscaster for a major network station.

Alvin Ailey Dance Theater is formed in New York.

1959 Berry Gordy, Jr. establishes Motown Records; Lorraine Hansberry's "A Raisin in the Sun" opens on Broadway.

1960 Civil Rights Act of 1960 introduces criminal penalties for obstructing the implementation of federal court orders and requires voting and registration records for federal elections be preserved.

College students in Greensboro, NC, stage sit-in to integrate the F.W. Woolworth lunch counter, sparking a wave of sit-ins throughout the South; Student Nonviolent Coordinating Committee (SNCC) formed at Shaw University in Raleigh, NC.

Harry Belafonte wins Emmy Award.

1961 Black and white Freedom Riders test federal laws integrating bus stations. Riders beaten and the bus bombed in Anniston, AL.

1962 At least eight black churches torched in the South for voter registration and other Civil Rights activities.

James Meredith, escorted by federal marshals, becomes the first black student to enter the University of Mississippi.

1963 Centennial celebration of the Emancipation Proclamation begins with voter registration in Greenwood, MS

250,000 participate in "March on Washington for Jobs, Justice, and Peace" at Lincoln Memorial. Martin Luther King, Jr. delivers his "I Have a Dream" speech.

Four black girls killed as bomb explodes Sunday morning in Sixteenth Street Baptist Church in Birmingham, AL.

Two black students integrate the University of Alabama, as Governor George Wallace tries to physically block their entry.

Ralph Bunche first black winner of the Presidential Medal of Freedom.

1964 Twenty-fourth Amendment eliminates poll tax, often used to keep African Americans in the South from voting.

President Johnson signs 1964 Civil Rights Act, prohibiting discrimination in public accommodations, facilities, and schools; also created the Equal Employment Opportunity Commission to monitor employment discrimination.

Congress passes Economic Opportunity Act, part of President Johnson's War on Poverty.

Three Civil Rights workers—two white, one black—murdered in Philadelphia, MS. Forty years later, one person is convicted of the lesser charge of manslaughter and sentenced to 60 years in prison.

The Mississippi Freedom Democratic Party (MFDP) delegation led by Fannie Lou Hamer is denied seating at the Democratic National Convention.

▲ Malcolm X publicly announces his break from the Nation of Islam.

1965 State troopers wielding billy clubs and tear gas attack civil rights marchers on Selma's Edmund Pettus Bridge on what became known as "Bloody Sunday."

Voting Rights Act of 1965 signed, suspending literacy tests and voter disqualification devices for five years and authorizing the use of federal examiners to supervise voter registration.

Malcolm X, also known as El-Hajj Malik El-Shabazz, assassinated in Audubon Ballroom in Harlem, NY.

1966 Robert Weaver sworn in as secretary of housing and urban development, the first African American cabinet member; Constance Baker Motley becomes first African-American woman appointed a federal judge.

Stokely Carmichael becomes chairman of SNCC and publicly

embraces the concept of black power; Huey Newton and Bobby Seale found Black Panther Party.

Maulana Karenga creates the festival Kwanzaa, celebrated between December 26 and January 1, to restore and reclaim African heritage and culture.

Edward Brooke (MA) first African American since Reconstruction elected to the U.S. Senate and first to be elected by popular vote.

1967 Thurgood Marshall appointed to the Supreme Court.

Loving v. Virginia strikes down state interracial marriage bans.

Riots erupt in 159 cities as African Americans lash out in frustration over long overdue civil rights.

Carl B. Stokes elected mayor of Cleveland, OH—first black mayor of a major U.S. city.

1968 Martin Luther King, Jr. assassinated in Memphis, TN. Supporters worldwide mourned.

SCLC President Rev. Ralph David Abernathy leads Poor People's Campaign to Washington, D.C. and builds Resurrection City near Lincoln Memorial.

Shirley Chisholm (NY) is the first African American woman elected to Congress.

Congress enacts the Civil Rights Act of 1968 which outlaws discrimination in the sale and rental of 80 percent of the housing in the U.S.

African Americans represent 9.8% of troops stationed in Vietnam, 20% of combat troops.

1969 SCLC leads more than 700 hospital workers in Charleston, SC in strike protesting discrimination.

1970 President Nixon signs 1970 Voting Rights Act Amendment, extending provisions of Voting Rights Act of 1965 to 1975.

1971 Congressional Black Caucus formed. As of 2011, 132 African Americans have served as U.S. Representatives or Senators.

Rev. Jesse Jackson forms People United to Serve Humanity (PUSH).

President Nixon rejects the 60 demands of the Congressional Black Congress.

▶ **1972** Barbara Jordan (TX) and Andrew Young (GA) become first black Congressional representatives elected from the Deep South since 1898.

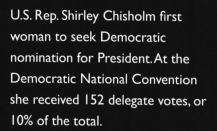

U.S. Rep. Shirley Chisholm first woman to seek Democratic nomination for President. At the Democratic National Convention she received 152 delegate votes, or 10% of the total.

1973 National Black Network, the nation's first black-owned radio news, begins broadcasting to 40 affiliates nationwide.

1974 Boston public schools ordered to integrate; national guard called in to restore order.

Hank Aaron breaks Babe Ruth's major league baseball record with his 715th home run. Before his

retirement in 1976 Aaron held the home run record, records for at-bats, total bases, extra-base hits, and runs batted in.

1975 National Association of Black Journalists formed.

National press reveals FBI and CIA conducted intensive spy campaigns on black leaders.

Voting Rights Act Amendment extends provisions of the 1965 Voting Rights Act to 1982; permanently bans literacy tests as requirements for voting.

1976 U.S. Rep. Barbara Jordan first African American to make the keynote speech at the Democratic National Convention; U. S. Rep. Andrew Young appointed U. S. Ambassador to the United Nations.

1977 Black colleges and universities experience major increase in enrollment, producing the largest African American student bodies at that time.

Television audience for *Roots*, based on Alex Haley's novel, largest in entertainment program history, with 130 million watching the eight-night presentation.

1978 Regents of the University of California v. Bakke rules that affirmative action is constitutional, but invalidates use of racial quotas.

1979 Weber v. Kaiser Aluminum and Chemical Corp rules that employers and unions can establish volunteer programs, including quotas, to aid minority employment.

Hazel W. Johnson first African American woman General in the United States Army.

1980 Supreme Court rules local elections cannot be declared unconstitutional unless intentional discrimination can be proven.

1981 Department of Justice announces it will no longer enforce busing to counteract desegregation in public schools.

1982 Voting Rights Act Amendment of 1982 extends Voting Rights Act of 1965 for 25 years; provides for bilingual election materials.

1983 Martin Luther King, Jr.'s birthday established as a federal holiday.

1985 Supreme Court rules affirmative action plans for state employment constitutional.

1986 Martin Luther King, Jr. bust unveiled in Great Rotunda of the United States Capitol.

1987 Supreme Court Justice Thurgood Marshall criticized plans for national celebration of bicentennial of the U.S. Constitution. He points out that the document excluded Blacks, native Americans and women.

1988 Presidential candidate Jesse Jackson wins five state primaries on Super Tuesday and urges "Keep Hope Alive."

1989 Ronald Brown first African American elected chairman of the Democratic Party.

Supreme Court rules white workers claiming reverse discrimination could seek redress.

Gen. Colin Powell named Chairman of Joint Chiefs of Staff, the highest military position held by an African-American.

1990 L. Douglass Wilder of Virginia first elected black governor.

1991 President George Bush signs "compromised" Civil Rights Bill, making it easier for workers to sue for job discrimination. It differed from the Civil Rights Act of 1866 which applied only to black employees, and gave whites the right to sue their employers for punitive and compensatory damages in cases of employment discrimination. Civil Rights leaders attack the law as an assault on decades of Civil Rights progress.

1992 Carol Moseley Braun (IL) first African American woman elected to the United States Senate.

1995 Million Man March.

1996 California voters pass Proposition 209, outlawing affirmative action in the state.

1998 President Bill Clinton appoints prominent historian John Hope Franklin to lead the President's Commission on Race.

2001 Gen. Powell appointed Secretary of State, first African American to hold this post.

2003 Grutter v. Bollinger upholds the University of Michigan Law School's admission policy which supports affirmative action.

Gratz v. Bollinger requires the University of Michigan to dismantle its affirmative action policy for undergraduate admissions.

2005 Condoleezza Rice first African American woman to hold the post of Secretary of State.

Barack Obama (IL) fifth African American to serve in the Senate.

2006 For the first time in U.S. history four African American members of Congress chair full committees in the House: Rep. John Conyers (MI), Judiciary, Rep. Juanita Millender McDonald (CA), House Administration Committee, Rep. Charles Rangel (NY), House Ways and Means, and Rep. Bennie G. Thompson (MS), Homeland Security.

Voting Rights Act of 2006 extends provisions of the 1965 Voting Rights Act for 25 years. Also extends the bilingual election requirements through August 5, 2032.

2007 The U.S. Supreme Court rules in Parents Involved in Community Schools v. Seattle School District No. 1, and Meredith v. Jefferson County (Kentucky) Board of Education, race cannot be a factor in the determination of school assignments.

▲ **2008** Sen. Obama first African American elected President of the U.S. He is sworn in January 2009 as the nation's 44th President.

2009 Former Maryland Lt. Governor Michael S. Steele becomes Chairman of Republican National Committee.

2013 Celebration of the 150th anniversary of the signing of the Emancipation Proclamation.

The Struggle for

One hundred years after the Emancipation Proclamation, more than 250,000 people gathered in Washington, D.C. on August 28, 1963, for the March on Washington, which was named by the organizers as a "Demonstration for Jobs and Freedom." Addressing a crowd that stretched from the Lincoln Memorial, the site that pays tribute to the "Great Emancipator," to the Washington Monument, Martin Luther King, Jr. delivered what has become known as his "I Have a Dream" speech, which began: "Five score years ago a great American in whose symbolic shadow we stand today signed the Emancipation Proclamation." [127]

While King's speech is well known, this is less known about the March on Washington: "The day was, in part, a massive lobbying effort for a new Emancipation Proclamation—which indeed within a year emerged as the 1964 Civil Rights Act from a Congress that could never have conceived of such a series of transformative laws even two years earlier." [128] King had persistently encouraged President John F. Kennedy to issue a "Second Emancipation" based on the first section of the 14th Amendment. A telegram dated December 13, 1961, from King to the President read: "WE URGE YOU ISSUE AT ONCE A SECOND EMANCIPATION PROCLAMATION TO FREE ALL NEGROES FROM SECOND CLASS CITIZENSHIP." [129] During a private tour of the White House, King had personally appealed to the President, who suggested King send him a draft. Lawyers for the Southern Christian Leadership Council (SCLC) submitted a document which Kennedy essentially ignored. Even so, the March on Washington was a high point in the Civil Rights movement, which was a hundred years in the making from Emancipation. Tragedies and triumphs loomed ahead. Many activists lost their lives, targeted by those hostile to black freedom who claimed the legacies of slavery—white entitlement and supremacy. Yet, in the slow, difficult onward flow of what Frederick Douglass called "the power of free speech, and national enlightenment," important legislation was successfully passed, bringing down the walls of segregation and prying open the voting booth. [130]

Fifty years after the March on Washington, America is a different place for black people. The black middle class has grown tremendously. More than ever, blacks have access to a college education and better job opportunities. But work remains to be done to close the gap between African Americans and other U.S. citizens in educational achievement and wealth, and to reverse one of the legacies of slavery—the overrepresentation of blacks in prison populations.

The vision that morning on January 1, 1863, when the Emancipation Proclamation was signed is still attainable, but requires constant vigilance. [131]

Freedom Continues

…words on a parchment would not be enough to deliver slaves from bondage, or provide men and women of every color and creed their full rights and obligations as citizens of the United States. What would be needed were Americans in successive generations who were willing to do their part—through protests and struggle, on the streets and in the courts, through a civil war and civil disobedience and always at great risk—to narrow that gap between the promise of our ideals and the reality of their time.

A MORE PERFECT UNION 3/18/08

We the people declare today that the most evident truth that all of us are created equal—is the star that guides us still; just as it guided our forebears through Seneca Falls and Selma and Stonewall; just as it guided all those men and women, sung and unsung, who left footprints along this great mall, to hear a preacher say that we cannot walk alone; to hear a King proclaim that our individual freedom is inextricably bound to the freedom of every soul on Earth.

SECOND INAUGURAL ADDRESS 1/21/13

The Civil War was one of the bloodiest in history, and yet it was only through the crucible of the sword, the sacrifice of multitudes, that we could begin to perfect this union and drive the scourge of slavery from our soil. **AGAINST THE IRAQ WAR 10/02**

This is the source of our confidence: the knowledge that God calls on us to shape an uncertain destiny. This is the meaning of our liberty and our creed, why men and women and children of every race and every faith can join in celebration across this magnificent mall. And why a man whose father less than 60 years ago might not have been served at a local restaurant can now stand before you to take a most sacred oath. **FIRST INAUGURAL ADDRESS 1/20/09**

. . . the unfinished legacy that calls us still—is a fundamental belief in the continued perfection of American ideals. It's a belief that says if this nation was truly founded on the principles of freedom and equality, it could not sit idly by while millions were shackled because of the color of their skin. **RFK HUMAN RIGHTS AWARD CEREMONY 11/16/05**

Washington
1889
NA

Montana
1889
NA

North Dakota
1889
NA

Oregon
1859
1844

Idaho
1890
NA

South Dakota
1889
NA

Wyoming
1890
NA

California
1850
1865

Nevada
1864
NA

Nebraska
1867
NA

Utah
1896
1863

Colorado
1876
NA

Kansas
1861
NA

Arizona
1912
NA

New Mexico
1912
NA

Oklah
19
N

Texas
1845
1865

Year the state was admitted to the union.

Year the last slaves in that state were freed.

NA Denotes that slavery was never legal in that state,
however see interesting information in "Slavery
State-by-State" on the next pages.

New Hampshire
1788 / **1783**

Vermont
1791 / **1777**

Maine
1820
NA

esota
858
NA

Wisconsin
1848
NA

West Virginia
1863 / **1863**

Massachusetts
1788 / **1783**

Michigan
1837
1830s

New York
1788 / **1841**

Rhode Island
1790 / **1842**

Iowa
1846
NA

Pennsylvania
1787 / **1847**

Connecticut
1788 / **1848**

Ohio
1803
1803

New Jersey
1787 / **1846**

Illinois
1818
NA

Indiana
1816
NA

Delaware
1787 / **1865**

Virginia
1788
1865

Maryland
1788 / **1865**

Missouri
1821
1865

Kentucky
1792 / **1865**

Washington DC
Not a state / **1862**

North Carolina
1789 / **1865**

Tennessee
1796 / **1865**

Arkansas
1836
1865

South Carolina
1788
1865

Georgia
1788
1865

Mississippi
1817
1865

Alabama
1819
1865

Louisiana
1812
1865

Florida
1845 / **1865**

Alaska
1959 / **NA**

Hawaii
1959 / **NA**

107

The End of Slavery For the Record

Transitioning enslaved black people to freedom was a complex process. Slavery did not exist only in the South; it was an American institution, legal when the United States was founded. And although the number of enslaved in the North declined after the Revolutionary War, the institution continued to exist well into the 1800s in many Northern states. Between 1777 and 1804, all states north of Maryland took steps that would eventually end slavery, but the route to freedom in these states was often gradual. Only slaves in Massachusetts, Vermont, and New Hampshire were emancipated relatively quickly. But even in those states, abolition measures were ambiguous and their implementation inconsistent. In Pennsylvania, New Jersey, New York, Connecticut and Rhode Island, state legislatures adopted gradual abolition legislation, which dismantled slavery over a period spanning half a century—the entire lifetime of a person in bondage.

Another common misconception is that the Emancipation Proclamation freed all the slaves at once. However, the presidential decree only declared all slaves in the Southern states free. It applied only to those enslaved in the eleven Confederate states, and since those states had seceded from the Union and formed their own government, they did not recognize the federal government's authority over them. Therefore, the actual "date" for emancipation also becomes complex.

The map on the previous page shows the date each state was admitted to the United States and the approximate date the last slaves were freed in that state. The Thirteenth Amendment to the Constitution, which prohibited slavery in the U.S., was ratified on December 6, 1865, so that is the date many states acknowledge as the end of slavery.

Alabama The Emancipation Proclamation declared the enslaved free, but it took Union victory in Civil War battles to actually free them. Alabama, a Confederate state, ratified the Thirteenth Amendment on December 2, 1865, and for a brief, progressive period, many anti-slavery whites and blacks were elected to state and congressional offices. However, by the end of 1874, pro-slavery forces had seized control of the legislature and governor's office, and instituted segregation that oppressed blacks politically, economically and socially.

Alaska The continental United States considered slavery as the bondage of Africans or their descendants, which in that form, never existed in Alaska. Indigenous people and some whites, however, did enslave Natives from other tribes. As late as 1903 there were still documented cases of such slavery in the state.

Arizona Comprised of land that was The Arizona Territory and part of The New Mexico Territory, Arizona became a state in 1912, more than 40 years after the Thirteenth Amendment was ratified. In what was the New Mexico Territory, Native Americans had a history of enslaving rival tribes. Few African-Americans were slaves there in 1860 when it formally

State-by-State

approved slavery. The month following the Emancipation Proclamation, on February 24, 1863, President Lincoln signed a bill establishing a provisional government for the new territory that abolished slavery in Arizona Territory, but not in the part that remained New Mexico Territory.

Arkansas was one of the 11 Confederate states that seceded from the Union and southwest Arkansas remained a Confederate holdout and perpetual stronghold of slavery until the last battles of the Civil War. The Thirteenth Amendment was ratified there on April 14, 1865.

California In 1849, the year before statehood, California's legislature voted to prohibit slavery, but it also limited the legal rights of African-Americans. The 1850 federal Fugitive Slave Act, which provided for the seizure and return of runaway slaves, also affected California and newspapers advertised the sale of slaves in 1852. Anti-black sentiment grew in the years before the Civil War, and the state legislature twice nearly passed Exclusion Laws, prompting many free blacks to immigrate to British Columbia. In 1870, the Fifteenth Amendment, granting black men the right to vote, was added to the U.S. Constitution despite failing to pass in Califor-

nia. The state ratified the Thirteenth Amendment on December 19, 1865.

Colorado had pro-Union and pro-Confederate factions in the territory before gaining statehood more than a decade after the Emancipation Proclamation and Civil War.

Connecticut One of the original colony states, Connecticut's legislature enacted a law to gradually abolish slavery in 1784, but did not completely end it until 1848. Such gradual manumission laws were common in Northern states. Rather than free slaves, Connecticut's law provided that children born to slaves after March 1, 1784, could not be held "in servitude" beyond the age of 25. An amendment in 1797 reduced it to 21.

Delaware A Border State and one of the original colony states, Delaware did not secede from the Union; therefore, the Emancipation Proclamation did not apply to slaves there. Delaware continued to allow slavery, even after the Civil War. Delaware's General Assembly rejected the Thirteenth Amendment on Feb 8, 1865, calling it an illegal extension of federal power over states. Even though slavery ended in Delaware in 1865, when the amendment went into effect across the nation, the state did

not ratify the Thirteenth Amendment until February 12, 1901.

District of Columbia On April 16, 1862, President Abraham Lincoln signed a bill, the District of Columbia Emancipation Act, which ended slavery in Washington, D.C., eight months before the Emancipation Proclamation. The law compensated slave owners, essentially purchasing the enslaved and setting them free.

Florida has a complex record of slavery, from its Spanish history of enslavement to its legacy as a refuge for runaway slaves, to the relationship between descendants of Africans and the Native American Seminoles. As a Confederate holdout, Florida ignored the Emancipation Proclamation, refusing to free slaves until Union armies liberated them in battle. The Thirteenth Amendment was ratified in Florida on December 28, 1865, and later reaffirmed on June 9, 1868.

Georgia An original colony state and a Confederate state that seceded from the Union, Georgia's long slave-holding history did not end suddenly or easily. Its liberation of more than 400,000 slaves began during the Civil War and continued well into 1865, as former slaves, former slaveholders, and the Union Army struggled to

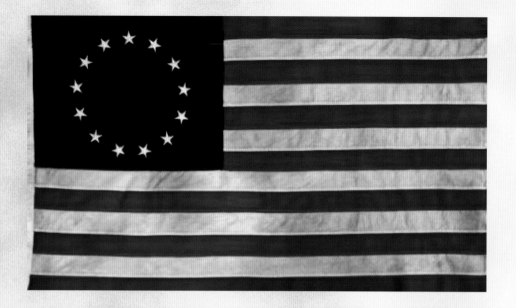

The thirteen original colony states

Connecticut	New York
Delaware	North Carolina
Georgia	Pennsylvania
Maryland	Rhode Island
Massachusetts	South Carolina
New Hampshire	Virginia
New Jersey	

enforce their respective visions of freedom. Georgia ratified the Thirteenth Amendment on December 6, 1865.

Hawaii The enslavement of Africans did not exist in Hawaii, but "kauwa", a system of serfdom similar to slavery did. It was abolished by the Hawaiian Kingdom in 1852: "Slavery shall, under no circumstances whatever, be tolerated in the Hawaiian Islands: whenever a slave shall enter Hawaiian territory he shall be free; no person who imports a slave, or slaves, into the King's dominions shall ever enjoy any civil or political rights in this realm; but involuntary servitude for the punishment of crime is allowable according to law…"

Idaho The Idaho Territory was created in 1863, the year of the Emancipation Proclamation. Prior to that, much of its land was considered part of Oregon, a free territory. Slavery was not permitted, however, blacks were excluded from settling through a series of laws enacted in the 1840s and 1850s.

In Idaho's territorial days, people with one-half or more Negro blood were prohibited from serving as witnesses, and those who were Negro or of mixed descent (black and white) were prohibited from marrying a white person. Few African descendants traveled west before the Civil War, and slave owners were reluctant to bring slaves to areas where laws upholding slavery might not be enforced or where the possibility of successful escape was great.

Illinois Lincoln's home state was a free state when it entered the Union in 1818, even though slavery was practiced. The state constitution preserved the rights of existing slaveholders, but appeased a Congress that did not wish to admit a slave-holding state. After, gaining statehood, the pro-slavery majority acted quickly to make it an active slave state. A system of indenture or "practical slavery" existed. Blacks that were technically free had unknowingly signed a work contract binding

them to someone white for a stated time period, for example, 99 years. This practice in Illinois constituted a limited form of slavery. Illinois was the first state to ratify the Thirteenth Amendment on February 1, 1865.

Indiana was granted statehood in 1816, when abolitionists were in control, and slavery and indenture were banned by state constitution. Opponents to slavery began to organize in the territorial legislature in 1805, overturning many of the laws that permitted slavery by 1809. In 1820, an Indiana Supreme Court ruling freed all remaining slaves in the state. In eastern Indiana, nearly all slaveholders immediately freed those they held in bondage. However, the majority of slaveholders in western counties, broke the law, hence the 1820 federal census, which lists 190 slaves in Indiana.

Hoosiers like Levi Coffin played important roles in the Underground Railroad, helping many slaves escape.

Abraham Lincoln lived in Indiana from 1816 until 1830, age 7 to 21, and first encountered and formed opinions about slavery from his experiences.

Many free blacks moving to Indiana settled along the Ohio River to work in the riverboat industry. Also, from 1820 to 1850, at least 30 black farm communities existed in central and southern Indiana. The 1850 census listed farming and farm labor as the most common occupations of blacks, but also listed other labor, service and domestic positions. Blacks were excluded from white society, including publicly funded schools; so they established their own schools, churches, and social organizations.

Proslavery/abolitionist tensions later resulted in increasing prejudice which culminated in the passage of Article XIII of the Indiana Constitution in 1851, which stated that "No negro or mulatto shall come into, or settle in the State..." and set fines for violations, providing that money collected from the fines be used to defray costs of sending blacks in Indiana to Liberia. Additional laws required all African Americans already living in the state to register with the circuit court. Indiana ratified the Thirteenth Amendment on February 13, 1865.

Iowa In 1839 "An Act to Regulate Blacks and Mulattoes" was passed by the first territorial legislature of Iowa. It required blacks to secure court certificates stating they were free and post a $500 bond as guarantee of good be-havior. (White nonfarm laborers at the time could expect to earn roughly 50 to 60 cents per day!) Employers who hired or harbored blacks who did not have a certificate were severely fined. Slaveholders could pass through Iowa with their slaves, and fugitive slaves were arrested and returned. In the early 1840s Indiana Quakers petitioned for repeal of the 1839 Act. The 1844 state constitution prohibited slavery, allowing blacks to settle in Iowa, but they could not vote, serve in the militia, or hold elected office.

Kansas was such a battleground between pro- and anti-slavery advocates that it was known as "Bleeding Kansas" when factions fought and killed one another over whether the territory would be slave or free. When it sought to enter the Union, another in a long series of compromises on slavery was negotiated in Congress. The Kansas-Nebraska Act of 1854 allowed whites in Kansas and Nebraska to decide for themselves whether to allow slavery within their borders. Several fraudulent elections resulted in the dispatch of federal troops to stop the violence. Congress then refused to recognize the constitution adopted by the pro-slavery settlers and Kansas was not allowed to become a state. Eventually anti-slavery settlers prevailed, drafted a new constitution, and on January 29, 1861—months before the Civil War—Kansas joined the Union as a free state.

Kentucky Kentucky was one of the slave-holding states that remained in the Union, exempt from the Emancipation Proclamation. Kentucky rejected the Thirteenth Amendment on Kentucky on February 24, 1865 and slaves there were legally freed more than 100 years later, when the state finally ratified the Thirteenth Amendment on March 18, 1976—the same year it also ratified the Fourteenth and Fifteenth Amendments.

Louisiana When slaves were freed by the Emancipation Proclamation, those in New Orleans and 13 named parishes of Louisiana were specifically exempted because most were already under Union control at the time. This left 300,000 slaves un-emancipated until the Thirteenth Amendment was ratified on February 17, 1865.

Maine Its application for statehood in 1819 was as a free, non-slave-holding state, but the complex balance of free and slave-holding states led to another famous compromise—the Missouri Compromise. Southern members of Congress threatened to prevent Maine from joining the Union if a balance between the numbers of slave and free states was not maintained. Missouri was admitted as a slave state, and Maine was admitted as a free state. Maine ratified the Thirteenth Amendment on February 7, 1865.

Maryland A Border State and one of the 13 original colony states, Maryland has a complicated history of slavery and emancipation. Maryland did not secede from the Union, therefore the

Many mistakenly believe that the Emancipation Proclamation abolished slavery in the entire U.S., but in fact, it only abolished slavery in the Confederate states.

Alabama	North Carolina
Arkansas	South Carolina
Florida	Tennessee
Georgia	Texas
Louisiana	Virginia
Mississippi	

Emancipation Proclamation did not free slaves there. Slavery continued legally until it was abolished when the state ratified the Thirteenth Amendment on February 3, 1865.

Massachusetts One of the original colony states, Massachusetts abolished slavery before it became one of the United States. A 1783 judicial decision, interpreting the wording of the 1780 state constitution, brought slavery to an end in Massachusetts. Although the constitution of 1780 was never amended to prohibit slavery, when courts refused to uphold slavery, it was doomed. Massachusetts was home to many staunch abolitionists.

Michigan During the French, British and early American periods of Detroit, many who could afford slaves had owned them, and in early 1700s Detroit during French rule, Native Americans were also enslaved. However, a growing abolitionist sentiment became more popular in the state. State laws banned slavery in the 1830s. Michigan became a center of the anti-slavery movement, and many residents were actively involved in helping fugitives as they sought freedom using the Underground Railroad.

Minnesota The U.S. Supreme Court's 1857 Dred Scott decision declared that as property, slaves were not citizens and could not sue to win their freedom even in non-slaveholding states. Although the decision outraged Minnesota abolitionists, it encouraged slave-holding tourists, politicians and soldiers to flock to the state, establishing a thriving pro-slavery economy. As many as 20 slaves came with vacationing Southerners in St. Cloud, the Twin Cities, and Stillwater. The 259 free blacks in Minnesota at the time of the state constitutional convention raised concerns far greater than their numbers would indicate, and inflamed debate about the legal and social status of the Negro.

Mississippi One of the Confederate states that seceded from the Union, Mississippi was forced to abolish slavery by the national ratification of the Thirteenth Amendment in 1865, but whites continued to suppress the social, political, and economic rights of former slaves. The first—and probably the harshest "Black Codes" were passed in Mississippi in November 1865, less than a year after the end of the Civil War.

Mississippi rejected the Thirteenth Amendment on December 4, 1865 and did not ratify it until March 16, 1995, thus making it the last state to officially ban slavery—130 years after the Amendment was passed by Congress.

Missouri A Border State that did not secede from the Union, Missouri's bid for statehood hinged on yet another famous compromise on slavery. According to the Missouri Compromise, it was admitted to the Union as a slave state and Maine was admitted as a free state to maintain a balance of slave-to-free states. But a stipulation was made that, in territory acquired through the Louisiana Purchase, slavery was outlawed above the 36° 30´ latitude and permitted below the line. That latitude line is at the base of Missouri, and all of the state is above the line, so the compromise set a geographic boundary for slavery but made Missouri the exception. It was to be the last area above the line where slavery was allowed in America's westward expansion.

Because, as a Border State, Missouri was exempt from the Emancipation Proclamation, slaves remained in bondage for two more years, until the state's own Emancipation Proclamation took effect on January 14, 1865. The state ratified the Thirteenth Amendment on February 6, 1865.

During the Civil War, because Lincoln's Emancipation Proclamation did not free slaves in Missouri, federal generals there faced a wartime challenge of attempting to distinguish runaway Missouri slaves from the newly freed slaves that inundated the state as they fled north from the Confederate states.

Montana became a state more than a decade after the Civil War, but during the War, as a part of the Dakota and Idaho territories, it had many white residents with strong ties to the slave-holding South and who opposed President Lincoln. Montana's first territorial governor was an abolitionist appointed by Lincoln, probably to assure the state maintained Union sympathy and to secure gold for the government to help finance the war. While federal officials tended toward abolitionism, the gold rush and defeat of the Confederate Army in Missouri brought pro-slavery Missourians to Montana. Evidence of their secessionist sentiments is revealed in the naming of Virginia City.

Nebraska Its history of slavery is part of the Kansas-Nebraska Act of 1854 that made it, like Kansas, a battleground in the Western territories between pro- and anti-slavery factions. This Act repealed the Missouri Compromise banning slavery above the geographic 36° 30´ latitude line, and allowed whites to vote on whether to allow or forbid slavery in their territory.

Nebraska was admitted to the Union in 1867 after the Civil War had ended slavery and the Thirteenth Amendment had been ratified. A clause in its proposed state constitution, limiting the right to vote to "free white males" delayed statehood for nearly a year.

Nevada Free blacks are an integral part of Nevada history. Jacob Dodson was a member of Fremont's explorers in the mid-1840s. Thousand of blacks, free and fugitives from slavery, arrived from the slave state of Texas to work in the cattle business as cowboys.

What became the state of Nevada was governed by the Congressional Compromise of 1850, which admitted California to the Union as a free state to satisfy abolitionists, strengthened the Fugitive Slave Act to appease pro-slavery forces, and left the issue of slavery to be decided by the territories of Nevada, New Mexico, Arizona, and Utah when they applied for statehood.

Nevada applied for and was granted statehood during the Civil War. It ratified the Thirteenth Amendment on February 16, 1865. African Americans organized after the end of the Civil War for united political action throughout the state and played a role in the celebration of the ratification of the Fifteenth Amendment on March 1, 1869.

Nevada's State Constitution excluded African Americans, Asians (whose numbers began to grow in the 1850s), and Native Americans from its system of compulsory education, despite the fact that such exclusions had not been part of its 1861 territorial legislation. A Nevada Supreme Court decision in 1872 opened the state's public education system to racial minorities.

New Hampshire Residents interpreted the Bill of Rights in its 1783 state constitution as prohibiting slavery, but in 1792, four years after New Hampshire became one of the original colony states, there were nearly 150 slaves there. Slavery was officially abolished in New Hampshire when it ratified the Thirteenth Amendment on July 1, 1865.

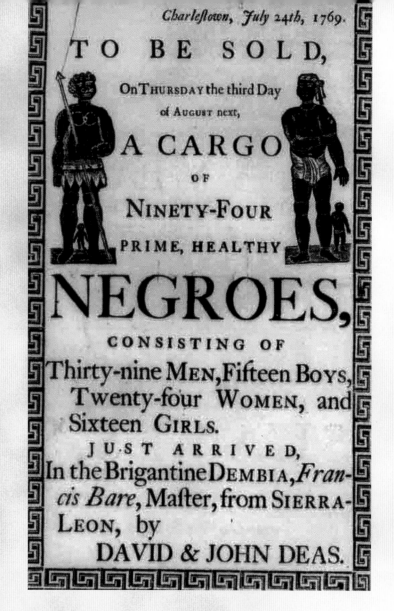

Charleftown, July 24th, 1769.

TO BE SOLD,

On Thursday the third Day of August next,

A CARGO

OF

NINETY-FOUR

PRIME, HEALTHY

NEGROES,

CONSISTING OF

Thirty-nine Men, Fifteen Boys, Twenty-four Women, and Sixteen Girls.

JUST ARRIVED,

In the Brigantine Dembia, *Francis Bare*, Master, from Sierra-Leon, by

DAVID & JOHN DEAS.

Slave-holding states where

the Emancipation Proclamation did NOT free slaves. When President Lincoln issued the Emancipation Proclamation, all slaves in the Confederacy were legally set free. Six slave-holding states, referred to as Border States, remained under Union control, so slaves in these states were not freed by the Proclamation.

Delaware   Tennessee (under Union occupation)

Kentucky   West Virginia (which was established as

Maryland   a free state in 1863)

Missouri

More than 40 percent of the Africans brought to the British colonies passed through South Carolina with Charleston as a major entry port for the Trans-Atlantic Slave Trade. On July 24, 1769, the firm David & John Deas created this broadside that advertised ninety-four healthy Africans arriving aboard the Brigantine Dembia to be sold at Charles Town (Charleston) on August 3. Although the Declaration of Independence proclaimed freedom as the right of every person, liberty was denied to captured Africans. The U.S. Constitution allowed the "Importation of such Persons" until 1808.

New Jersey An original colony state, New Jersey began gradual abolition of slavery in 1804 by freeing the children of slaves. Of the 3,568 blacks in the North who remained enslaved in 1830, more than two-thirds were in New Jersey. The state abolished slavery in 1846, but redefined former slaves as apprentices who were "apprenticed for life" to their masters. At the start of the Civil War, 18 "apprentices" were listed in the U.S. census as "slaves." Thus slavery continued in New Jersey without it technically being a slave state. New Jersey rejected the Thirteenth Amend-ment on March 16, 1865, but ratified it ten months later, on January 23, 1866.

New Mexico became a state in 1912, more than 30 years after the Thirteenth Amendment ending slavery had been adopted. (See Arizona.)

New York One of the original colony states, New York had the second largest slave population in the 1700s. New York gradually abolished slavery through a complex set of laws that finally freed its last slaves in 1841. In 1817, New York set a date of July 4, 1827, to completely phase out slavery. By 1828, the state had abolished slavery entirely, however, children born between 1799 and 1827 were deemed indentured servants until age 25 for females, and age 28 for males. Even then, slavery was not entirely repealed, because a law provided an exception allowing nonresidents to enter New York with slaves for up to nine months, and permitting part-time residents to bring slaves into the state temporarily. The "nine-months law" remained on the books until it was repealed in 1841. New York ratified the Thirteenth Amendment on February 3, 1865.

North Carolina An original colony state and a Confederate state that seceded from the Union, it was only after Union victory in Civil War battles that those in bondage were freed. Unlike other states that refused to validate the Thirteenth Amendment, North Carolina ratified it on December 4, 1865, nominally ending slavery there. But as with other Southern states, ratification was followed with a set of circumscribed laws and violent practices that suppressed the social, political, and economic rights of former slaves.

North Dakota Expansion in large numbers into the Northern Plains began during the Civil War when Congress organized the Dakota Territory, as railways were built, and the 1862 Federal Homestead Law promoted farming settlement. The settlement "boom" from 1879 to 1886 came decades after slavery had been abolished, and brought more than 100,000 ethnically varied people to the territory. While Norwegians were the largest group, Asians, Blacks, and Arabs also settled in North Dakota.

Ohio During the late 1700s and the early 1800s, prior to Ohio's statehood, many blacks lived with friendly Native Americans, since whites feared Native Americans and would not pursue runaway slaves among them. Ohio's first constitution in 1803 outlawed slavery. Although African descendants were among the first non-indigenous residents of Ohio and most were free, they were not allowed full citizenship.

Blacks could not vote, attend public schools, serve in the military or on juries, testify in court against whites, or receive public assistance. Black Laws were enacted in 1804 and 1807 that required blacks to post a prohibitively expensive bond guaranteeing good behavior and to show proof of their freedom to enter the state. The Exclusion Laws remained until 1849, when the Black Laws were partially repealed, but schools for black and white children remained separate and courts upheld segregation in 1850 and 1859.

While many whites supported laws that actively discouraged black settlement in Ohio, many other whites were active in the vibrant Underground Railroad in Ohio that assisted thousands of fugitive slaves to freedom.

Oklahoma Native Americans sometimes were slaveholders. Slavery was abolished in Indian Territory (now Oklahoma) on July 10, 1866 when the last of the Five Nations tribes signed a treaty to free their slaves.

Oregon Many whites brought slaves with them across the Oregon Trail, usually a longtime servant or a family deemed able to survive the harsh trip. Although the Oregon Provisional Government declared slavery illegal in 1844, it was not an abolitionist motive; it was a measure intended to keep the black population in Oregon to a minimum. Likewise, Exclusion Laws were passed in 1848, but repealed in 1854. The 1850 Oregon Donation Land Act granted free land to whites and half-

breed Indians, excluding blacks from land claims.

Pro-slavery forces agitated repeatedly to form a new territory from southwestern Oregon and northern California, which could eventually become a new slave state. An 1857 bill was introduced in the Territorial Legislature to protect the property of slave owners, which would have legalized slavery again by allowing slaveholders to keep blacks in bondage after moving to the Oregon Territory. The bill was defeated. Statehood followed the next year, with many proponents of slavery elected as the first state legislators.

In 1859, Oregon was the first state admitted to the Union with an Exclusion Law written into its state constitution, and in 1862 while the Civil War raged, Oregon adopted a law placing an annual tax on all blacks, Asians and individuals of mixed race. The Thirteenth Amendment was ratified on December 8, 1865; while the Fourteenth Amendment, granting citizenship to blacks did not pass until 1868. In 1870, the Fifteenth Amendment, granting black men the right to vote, was added to the U.S. Constitution despite its failure to pass in Oregon.

Pennsylvania An original colony state, Pennsylvania adopted measures for gradually phasing out slavery by 1847. Fewer than 100 slaves were recorded in the state census in 1840. The home of the Quakers, Pennsylvanians were powerful advocates for abolition.

Rhode Island In February 1784,

the legislature in this original colony state passed a compromise measure for gradual emancipation: Children of slaves born after March 1, 1784 were to be "apprentices." Females would become free at age 18, and males at 21. As with other laws involving gradual emancipation in the North, this gave slave owners many years of free labor. None of the enslaved were emancipated outright. The 1800 census listed 384 slaves in Rhode Island; and only five in 1840, after which slaves were no longer counted among the state census.

An essential element of the 1784 Compromise gave Rhode Island ship owners the right to continue participating in the foreign slave trade. In the early 19th century, residents turned to the old New England custom of "warning out" strangers to purify themselves racially. This practice involved evicting poor and undesirable strangers from the community. Blacks were increasingly targets, disproportionate to their numbers and without regard to whether they were long-term residents.

South Carolina One of the original colony states, South Carolina had a unique relationship to the United States. It was home to one of the most vocal pro-slavery U. S. Senators, John C. Calhoun, who in the 1830s, argued unsuccessfully that states had the right to refuse to enforce federal laws that were not beneficial to them. State legislators were the first to threaten to secede from the Union when Lincoln was elected, and the first to actually meet

to consider the question and vote overwhelmingly to do so.

Other Southern state legislative bodies followed South Carolina's lead in leaving the Union and creating a new country, the Confederate States of America. It resisted freeing those in bondage until forced to do so by battles of the Civil War and then, despite the influential role of black legislators during Reconstruction, eventually suppressed the social, political and economic rights of former slaves. South Carolina ratified the Thirteenth Amendment on November 13, 1865.

South Dakota The first African Americans in the Northern Great Plains were fur traders in the early 1800s. As part of the Dakota and Idaho territories, the land that became South Dakota experienced white immigration in large numbers during the Civil War, escalating in the early 1880s, decades after slavery had been abolished.

Tennessee joined the Confederacy and seceded from the U.S., but was also one of the six slave-holding Border States that remained under the control of the Union Army, and therefore exempt from Emancipation Proclamation. Tennessee ratified the Thirteenth Amendment on April 7, 1865, but in 1869, became the first in a succession of Southern states to establish an all-white "redeemer" government sympathetic to the cause of the Confederacy.

Texas was one of the last areas of the Confederacy to free those held in

bondage. While slaves there were actually emancipated on January 1, 1863, Union General Gordon Granger did not formally announce freedom in the state until June 19, 1865. (See "Juneteenth") The Thirteenth Amendment was ratified on February 18, 1870.

Utah Free blacks came to Utah during the exploration and fur-trapping period, as early as 1824. James P. Beckwourth and other Blacks arrived long before Mormon settlement in 1847 and three Black men listed as servants (Green Flake, Oscar Crosby and Hark Lay) arrived with the initial Mormon pioneer group. The 1850 census of Utah Territory counts 50 blacks: 24 free, and 26 enslaved. In a newspaper article from 1899, blacks were quoted as comparing their servitude in Utah as being as cruel as that on any plantation.

In early 1852 Brigham Young, Utah's first territorial governor, asked the legisture to give legal sanction to slavery, saying that although Utah was not suited for slavery the practice was ordained by God. On February 4, 1852, the territorial legislature passed "An Act in Relation to Service," which legally recognized slavery. Utah became the only territory west of the Missouri River and north of the Missouri Compromise line of 36°30' to legalize slavery. The Act also enumerated the responsibilities of slave and master.

While some masters emancipated slaves before the Emancipation Proclamation, most did so only after the law abolished slavery. Utah achieved statehood in1896, three decades after ratification of the Thirteenth Amendment.

Vermont Founders of Vermont, in breaking away from New York in 1777, abolished slavery outright in the state constitution on July 8, 1777. When the 1870 U.S. Census reported that there were 16 slaves in Bennington County, Vermont in 1790, the chief clerk at the time said it was a mistake. He changed the designation to "Free Other," allowing Vermont to keep its claim of being the first state to abolish slavery.

Virginia One of the original 13 states and home to men who represented the country's founding ideals, Virginia was a slave-holding state from its beginning and Richmond became the seat of the Confederacy. Even so, it was the first former Confederate State to ratify the Thirteenth Amendment, on February 9, 1865, two months before General Lee's surrender at Appomattox Courthouse in Virginia.

Washington Blacks are documented as early as 1852 in Washington. Some crossed the Western plains from Missouri intending to settle in Oregon, only to discover Exclusion Laws prohibiting them from living there. Washington then became their destination.

When the Civil War began in 1861, a west coast movement to establish a "Pacific Confederacy" was firmly squelched and the Washington Territorial Legislature passed an affirmation of loyalty to the Union. During the War, Washington Territorial volunteers enlisted for the Union; they served in Army posts in the region that freed soldiers to fight the Confederates. In the early 1870s the Northern Pacific Railroad brought increased immigration of various ethnic groups, including blacks. Before statehood, the Washington Territorial Legislature asked Congress to pass a law excluding Chinese laborers from the United States.

West Virginia was formed in 1861 as loyal to the Union, after voters west of the Allegheny Mountains rejected Virginia's secession from the U.S. West Virginia was formally established as a free state in 1863, during the Civil War.

Slavery was among the constitutional issues addressed. Because it was not yet a state when the Emancipation Proclamation was issued, slaves there were not automatically freed. Instead, after lengthy debate, a compromise known as the Wiley Agreement was reached. Under this convoluted agreement, no slaves were freed when West Virginia became a state, none would be released from bondage until 1867, and slaves aged 21 years and older would never be freed. Fortunately, the Thirteenth Amendment, which the state ratified on February 3, 1865, superseded those provisions.

Wisconsin was never a slave state, and its first legislators included abolitionists. Many residents were devoted to the cause of emancipation as active participants in the Underground Railroad.

A black man is documented to have participated in the first election held in Milwaukee in 1835, and the state constitution drafted in 1846 provided voting rights to African Americans. However voters rejected it, and the final constitution adopted for statehood did not specifically address the issue. While the majority approved Black suffrage in a subsequent referendum, voting rights continued to be denied until passage of the Fifteenth Amendment in 1869.

Wyoming In 1864, while the Civil War raged, and the year following the Emancipation Proclamation, whites in Wyoming broke the U.S. treaty with Native Americans by occupying Indian Territory. As more immigrants arrived, American Indian lands were further encroached. The resulting military conflict continued until 1876. In 1885, rioting occurred between Chinese and white immigrant miners, which resulted in the deaths of at least 28 Chinese miners and many Chinese homes being burned.

Tension between whites and Chinese, and whites and Native Americans dominated Wyoming in the decades during and following the Civil War, so while it was never a slave state, legal repression of non-whites was common. Marriage between whites and "Negroes, Mulattos, Mongolians, or Malaya" was illegal, and separate schools were mandated when there were 15 or more colored children within any school district.

About the Authors

Project advisor and writer Kevin McGruder is an Assistant Professor of History at Antioch College, Yellow Springs, Ohio. His research interests include African American institutions, urban history, gay and lesbian history, and public history. A native of Toledo, Ohio, McGruder has a B.A. in Economics from Harvard University and an M.B.A. in Real Estate Finance from Columbia Business School. He received his doctorate in U.S. History from the Graduate Center of the City University of New York. Before pursuing doctoral studies, McGruder worked for many years in the field of nonprofit community development. Positions included Program Director at Local Initiatives Support Corporation, and Director of Real Estate Development with the Abyssinian Development Corporation.

McGruder's interest in Harlem's history led to two entrepreneurial ventures. From 1990 to 1991 he was owner/manager of Home to Harlem, a gift shop with items celebrating Harlem. From 2000 to 2008 he was co-owner of Harlemade Style Shop, a store providing Harlem-themed T-shirts, books and other items.

His publications include "Pathologizing Sexuality: The U.S. Experience," in *Black Sexualities: Powers, Passions, Practices, and Policies*, edited by Sandra L. Barnes and Juan Battle (Rutgers University Press, 2010) and "To Be Heard in Print: Black Gay Writers in 1980s New York," *Obsidian III: Literature in the African Diaspora, Spring/Summer 2005, Volume 6, Number 1* (North Carolina State University).

He can be reached at kmcgruder@antiochcollege.org

Creative director Georgia Scott is a visual journalist, author, educator, media consultant, cultural scholar, and serial traveler. She worked at *The New York Times* for 15 years, including five months in Paris at *The International Herald Tribune*. She was a Knight Fellow in Indonesia and China, through the International Center for Journalists, and consultant on local journalism in Burma and Ecuador for American Embassies. As an educator, she is an Adjunct Professor (of Journalism and Media Communications) at the City University of New York.

Georgia is the author of three books. *Headwraps: A Global Journey* (Public Affairs, 2003), is a beautifully designed hardcover on the significance and lore of headwraps and head scarves around the world. In 2010, she published *How Langston*

Project writer and image researcher Velma Maia Thomas is the author of several nonfiction books on African American history, including the award-winning interactive *Lest We Forget: The Passage from Africa to Slavery and Emancipation* (Random House, 1997). Additional books in the series are *Freedom's Children*, *No Man Can Hinder Me*, and *We Shall Not Be Moved*. Maia served as manager of the Shrine of the Black Madonna Bookstore and Cultural Center in Atlanta, Georgia, from 1987 to 2000, where she created the nationally acclaimed Black Holocaust Exhibit, a collection of original documents on slavery in America.

A gifted writer and public historian, Maia was one of 100 distinguished Americans selected to contribute to *Lift Every Voice and Sing: A Celebration of the Negro National Anthem* (Random House, 2000). She also was selected to write the introduction to *Finding a Place Called Home: A Guide to African-American Genealogy and Historical Identity* (Random House, 1999). Her latest work, *The Odd Fellow City: The Promise of a Leading Black Town*, has been published in the 2012 edition of the *Journal of the Georgia Association of Historians*. Early this year, she served as a subject expert for the PBS documentary, *Underground Railroad: The William Still Story*, which aired nationally in February.

Maia holds a bachelor's degree in journalism from Howard University, a master's degree in political science from Emory University, and a graduate level certificate in Heritage Preservation from Georgia State University. She has served as keynote speaker at universities, libraries and museums across the nation and has served as a distinguished scholar at the historic Penn Center on St. Helena Island, South Carolina. Maia has been interviewed by *The New York Times*, *The Atlanta Journal and Constitution*, and the British Broadcasting Corporation. She continues to write, teach, and speak on African American history, using her engaging style to bring history to life.

She can be reached at vmaiathomas@hotmail.com

Leaf Delayed Winter, an illustrated children's book.

Georgia holds a bachelor's degree in visual journalism from Grambling State University. She has traveled to 57 countries and speaks three languages (some better than others). She strongly advocates cross-cultural understanding, and was reignited with deep passion and heartbreak over the many nuances of cultural conflict during America's path to racial equality while working on this project.

She can be reached at georgiaworldwide@gmail.com

One of the greatest human freedoms is choosing those with whom we work. The team for this book was choice:

Nira Hyman, **Evette Porter**, and **Grace Ali** — copy editors, of whom **Waheedah Bilal** was super copy chief;

Dennis Palmore, rights hero;

Natalie Renee Perkins, Bible interpreter; and

Sandra Jamison, intrepid researcher.

Thank you all!

Endnotes

1. Abraham Lincoln, "Emancipation Proclamation" (Madison, Wisconsin: Martin & Judson, 1864)

2. James Lantos, Thomas Jefferson, 1734–1826 (Carlisle, MA: Applewood Books, 2009) 6

3. John Locke, Two Treatises of Government (London: Whitmore and Fenn, and C. Brown, 1821) 234; The American Colonization Society, The African Repository and Colonial Journal, Volume 12 (Washington, DC: Way and Gideon, 1836) 378

4. Carol Berkin, A Brilliant Solution: Inventing the American Constitution (New York: Harcourt, Inc., 2002)

5. Stephen L. Schecter and Richard B. Bernstein, eds., Roots of the Republic: American Founding Documents Interpreted, Issue 2 (Blue Ridge Summit, PA: Rowman and Littlefield, 1991) 236

6. Schecter and Bernstein 269; Berkin, 42; John K. Alexander, The Selling of the Constitutional Convention: A History of News Coverage (Blue Ridge Summit, PA: Rowman and Littlefield, 1990) 65–71

7. James Madison, Notes of the Debates in the Federal Convention of 1787 (New York: W.W. Norton, 1985) 504

8. Eli Ginzberg and Alfred C. Eichner, Troublesome Presence: Democracy and Black Americans (Piscataway, NJ: Transaction Publishers, 1993) 57

9. David Brian Robertson, The Constitution and America's Destiny (Cambridge University Press, 2005) 283; Schecter and Bernstein, 266–290

10. Carol Berkin, A Brilliant Solution: Inventing the American Constitution (New York: Harcourt, Inc., 2002)

11. David O. Stewart, The Summer of 1787:The Men Who Invented the Constitution, (New York: Simon & Schuster, 2007) 206

12. "Africans Came with Columbus to New World" http://www.livescience.com/3423-africans-columbus-world.

html; Junius P. Rodriguez, Slavery in the United States: A Social, Political, and Historical Encyclopedia (Santa Barbara, CA: ABC-CLIO, 2007) 6, 45; Leslie Harris, In the Shadow of S20y: African Americans in New York City:1626–1863 (University of Chicago, 2004) 12–13

13. John Thornton, The African Experience of the "20 and Odd Negroes" Arriving in Virginia in 1619, The William and Mary Quarterly, Third Series, Vol. 55, No. 3 (Jul., 1998) 421–434

14. Franklin E. Grizzard and D. Boyd Smith, Jamestown Colony: A Political, Social, and Cultural History, (Santa Barbara, CA: ABC-CLIO) 198; Rodriguez, 6; http://www.swarthmore.edu/SocSci/bdorsey1/41docs/24-sla.html.

15. Suzanne Miers and Igor Kopytoff, eds., Slavery in Africa: Historical and Anthropological Perspectives (Madison: University of Wisconsin, 1979) 5–6; Malyn Newitt, A History of Portuguese Overseas Expansion, 1400–1668 (East Sussex, England: Psychology Press, 2004) 25–29

16. Philip Morgan, Slave Counterpoint: Black Culture in the Eighteenth Century Chesapeake and Lowcountry (Chapel Hill, NC: University of North Carolina 1998) 27–58

17. Faith Berry, From Bondage to Liberation: Writings by and about Afro-Americans (New York: Continuum International Publishing Group, 2006) 24; Pennsylvania Society for Promoting the Abolition of Slavery, Edward Needles, An historical memoir of the Pennsylvania Society for promoting the Abolition of Slavery, the Release of Free Negroes Unlawfully Held in Bondage (Philadelphia: Merrihew and Thompson, 1848) 14–15

18. Justin Buckley Dyer, Natural Law and the Antislavery Constitutional Tradition (New York: Cambridge University Press, 2012) 119; Angela Lakwete, Inventing the Cotton Gin: Machine and Myth in Antebellum America (Baltimore: Johns Hopkins University Press, 2005) 76; Ira Berlin,

Many Thousands Gone: The First Two Centuries of Slavery in North America (Cambridge, MA: Harvard University Press, 1998) 142–176; William J. Cooper, Jr., The South and the Politics of Slavery, 1828–1856 (Baton Rouge: Louisiana State University Press, 1980) 370

19. M. Alpha Bah, "Legitimate Trade, Diplomacy and the Slave Trade" in Africana Studies: A Survey of Africa and the African Diaspora, ed. Mario Azevedo (Durham, NC: Carolina Academic Press, Third Edition, 2005) 71–89; Philip D. Curtin, The Atlantic Slave Trade: A Census (Madison: University of Wisconsin Press, 1969) 276

20. John Cummings and Joseph Adna Hill, Negro Population in the United States, 1790–1915 By United States. Bureau of the Census (Washington, DC: U.S. Census Office, Department of the Interior, 1968) 53; James Madison Edmunds, Statistics of the United States (Washington, DC: U.S. Census Office, Department of the Interior, 1860) 337.

21. Josef Raab, Dr. Martin Butler, eds., Hybrid Americas: Contacts, Contrasts, and Confluences in New World Literatures and Cultures (London: LIT Verlag Münster, 2008) 21–144

22. Floyd Calvin Shoemaker, Missouri's Struggle for Statehood, 1804–1821 (Jefferson City, MO: Hugh Stephens Printing Co., 1916) 39, 11–134

23. Kirkpatrick Sale, The Fire of His Genius: Robert Fulton and the American Dream (New York: Simon and Schuster, 2002) 91–92; Richard G. Lipsey, Kenneth I. Carlaw and, Clifford T. Bekar, Economic Transformations: General Purpose Technologies and Long-Term Economic Growth (New York: Oxford University Press, 2006) 182–188; David R. Meyer, The Roots of American Industrialization (Baltimore: John Hopkins University Press, 2003); Stanley L. Engerman, Slavery, Emancipation and Freedom: Comparative Perspectives (Baton Rouge, LA: Louisiana State University Press, 2007)

24. Thomas DeWolf, Inheriting the

Trade: A Northern Family Confronts Its Legacy as the Largest Slave-Trading Dynasty in U.S. History (Boston: Beacon Press, 2008) 58–61

25. Karl Jack Bauer and Robert W. Johannsen, The Mexican War, 1846-1848 (Lincoln, NE: University of Nebraska Press, 1992); John C. Waugh, On the Brink of Civil War: The Compromise of 1850 and How It Changed the Course of American History (Lanham, MD: Rowman and Littlefield, 2003) 177–184

26. William R. Black, Transportation: A Geographical Analysis (New York: Guilford Press, 2003) 21; Armando Navarro, The Immigration Crisis: Nativism, Armed Vigilantism, and the Rise of a Countervailing Movement (Lanham, MD: Rowman Altamira, 2008) 20; James Dunwoody Brownson Debow, The Seventh Census of the United States: 1850, An Appendix (Washington, DC: R. Armstrong, 1853) xxxviii, ixxxviii.

27. Michael R. Haines and Richard Hall Steckel, A Population History of North America (Cambridge: Cambridge University Press, 2000) 435; DeBow, Statistical View of the United States (Washington, DC: United States. Census Office, 1850) 95, 99

28. Deborah Goodrich Bisel, The Civil War in Kansas: Ten Years of Turmoil (Charleston, SC: The History Press, 2012)

29. http://www.encyclopedia.com/topic/Middle_Passage.aspx

30. http://nationalhumanitiescenter.org/pds/amerbegin/exploration/text7/text7read.htm

31. http://slaverebellion.org/index.php?page=united-states-insurrections

32. http://www.pbs.org/wnet/slavery/timeline/1619.html

33. http://www.aaregistry.org/historic_events/view/first-black-birth-recorded-america

34. http://www.understandingrace.org/history/gov/colonial_authority.html

35. http://www.pbs.org/wnet/slavery/timeline/1662.html

36. http://www.pbs.org/wgbh/aia/part1/1p268.html

37. http://www.pbs.org/wgbh/aia/part2/2h70t.html

38. http://www.archives.gov/exhibits/charters/declaration.html

39. https://www.nyhistory.org/web/africanfreeschool/history/manumission-society.html

40. http://www.academicamerican.com/revolution/documents/northwestord.htm

41. http://www.archives.gov/philadelphia/exhibits/franklin/slavery.html

42. http://www.pbs.org/wgbh/aia/part3/3h511.html

43. http://www.pbs.org/wgbh/aia/part4/4p1561.html

44. http://historymatters.gmu.edu/d/6811/

45. Bruce Wetterau, The New York Public Library Book of Chronologies (New York, NY: Macmillan, 1990)

46. http://www.britannica.com/EBchecked/topic/19269/American-Anti-Slavery-Society

47. http://www.pbs.org/wnet/slavery/timeline/1837.html

48. http://memory.loc.gov/ammem/aaohtml/exhibit/aopart1b.html#01d

49. http://www.blackpast.org/?q=1843-henry-highland-garnet-address-slaves-united-states

50. Kwame Anthony Appiah and Henry Louis Gates Jr. eds., Africana: The Encyclopedia of the African and African American Experience (New York, NY: Basic Civitas Books, 1999)

51. http://www.nationalcenter.org/FugitiveSlaveAct.html

52. Bruce Wetterau, The New York Public Library Book of Chronologies (New York, NY: Macmillan, 1990)

53. http://www.ushistory.org/us/31a.asp

54. Bruce Wetterau, The New York Public Library Book of Chronologies (New York, NY: Macmillan, 1990)

55. Kwame Anthony Appiah and Henry Louis Gates Jr. eds., Africana: The Encyclopedia of the African and African

American Experience (New York, NY: Basic Civitas Books, 1999)

56. http://www.encyclopediavirginia.org/Carter_Robert_1728-1804

57. http://www.davemanuel.com/inflation-calculator.php

58. http://www.loc.gov/exhibits/odyssey/educate/truth.html

59. http://www25.uua.org/uuhs/duub/articles/lydiamariachild.html

60. http://www.harrietbeecherstowe-center.org/hbs/

61. http://www.ohiohistorycentral.org/entry.php?rec=84

62. http://www.pbs.org/wgbh/aia/part2/2p39.html

63. http://www.pbs.org/wgbh/aia/part4/4h2933t.html

64. http://www.blackpast.org/?q=1843-samuel-h-davis-we-must-assert-our-rightful-claims-and-plead-our-own-cause

65. The Gabriel Prosser Slave Revolt. Retrieved from http://msuweb.montclair.edu/~furrg/spl/gabrielrevolt.html

66. Junius P. Rodriguez, ed.,Slavery in the United States: A Social, Political and Historical Encyclopedia, Vol. 1, (ABC-CLIO Inc., Santa Barbara, Ca., 2007) 29. Retrieved from http://books.google.com/books?id=4X44KbDBl9gC&pg=RA1-PA29&lpg=RA1-PA29&dq=gabriel+prosser+and+Virginia+abolitionists&source=bl&ots=IuV5Wq-dUW&sig=SreO5jHYOgcMtT-4gPzjYiS-AhZA&hl=en&sa=X&ei=fwMpU28J4e60QHEpYHIDA&ved=0CFYQ6AEwCTgK#v=onepage&q=gabriel%20pross]

67. Nat Turner's Rebellion retrieved from http://www.pbs.org/wgbh/aia/part3/3p1518.html

68. http://memory.loc.gov/ammem/aaohtml/exhibit/aopart1b.html

69. http://law2.umkc.edu/faculty/projects/ftrials/trialheroes/Tappanessay.html

70. Ibid.

71. Ibid.

72. Letter Home by John A. Copeland (1859), retrieved from http://www.oberlin.edu/archive/exhibits/john_brown/page3.html

73. Life and Times of Frederick Douglass, retrieved from http://www2.iath.virginia.edu/jbrown/fdlife.html

74. Dangerfield Newby's Letters from His Wife, Harriet retrieved from http://www.lva.virginia.gov/public/trailblazers/res/Harriet_Newby_Letters.pdf

75. Dangerfield Newby: A Tragic Journey to Harpers Ferry, retrieved from http://www.hmdb.org/marker.asp?marker=50611

76. William Lloyd Garrison, "The Great Crisis," The Liberator Vol. II. No. 52 (December 29, 1832)

77. Frank Moore, The Rebellion Record: A Diary of American Events (New York: Nabu Press) 166–75, quoted on 118; Kenneth Milton Stampp, The Causes of The Civil War (Englewood Cliffs, N.J.: Prentice-Hall, Inc. 1974)

78. E.B. Long with Barbara Long, The Civil War Day by Day: An Almanac, 1861–1865, (Garden City, New York: Doubleday & Company, Inc. 1971), 200. Note, on April 21, 1962 certain exemptions were granted, 202

79. Thomas G. Mitchell, Anti-Slavery Politics in Civil War and Ante-Bellum America (Santa Barbara, CA: Greenwood Publishing Group, 2007) 78

80. William E. Glenapp, The Origins of the Republican Party, 1852–1856 (New York, N.Y.: Oxford University Press, 1988) 413–443

81. Bruce Chadwick, 1858: Abraham Lincoln, Jefferson Davis, Robert E. Lee, Ulysses S. Grant and the War They Failed to See, (Napierville, IL: Sourcebooks, 2011) 98

82. Abraham Lincoln and Stephen Arnold Douglas, The Lincoln-Douglas Debates of 1858, Volume 3 (Springfield, IL: Trustees of the Illinois State Historical Library, 1908) 100

83. Abraham Lincoln and Stephen Arnold Douglas, The Lincoln-Douglas Debates of 1858, Volume 3 (Springfield, IL: Trustees of the Illinois State His-torical Library, 1908) 96 http://www.sonofthesouth.net/slavery/abraham-lincoln/lincoln-douglas-debate.htm

84. Michael S. Green, Lincoln and the Election of 1860 (Carbondale, IL: Southern Illinois University Press, 2011) 88–114

85. Abraham Lincoln and Stephen Arnold Douglas, The Lincoln-Douglas Debates of 1858, Volume 3 (Springfield, IL: Trustees of the Illinois State Historical Library, 1908) 100; Barry Sanders and Francis Adams, Alienable Rights: The Exclusion of African Americans in a White Man's Land (New York: HarperCollins, 2004) 136–166

86. Barry Sanders, Francis Adams, Alienable Rights: The Exclusion of African Americans in a White Man's Land (New York: HarperCollins, 2004) 180–185; Emory M. Thomas, The Confederate State of Richmond: A Biography of the Capital (Baton Rouge, LA: Louisiana State University Press, 1998) 3–32

87. William J. Cooper, We Have the War Upon Us: The Onset of the Civil War, November 1860-April 1861 (New York: Random House Digital, 2012) 268–270

88. Robert Cowley and Geoffrey Parker, The Reader's Companion to Military History (New York: Houghton Mifflin, 2001) 15–19

89. James M. McPherson, ed., We Cannot Escape History: Lincoln and the Last Best Hope of Earth (Champaign: University of Illinois Press, 2011) 77–80; [Jim Downs, Sick from Freedom: African-American Illness and Suffering during the Civil (New York: Oxford University Press, 2012) 45–52

90. Philip S. Foner, The Life and Writings of Frederick Douglass, Vol. III (New York: International Publishers, 1952) 244–46

91. Michael Linfield, Freedom Under Fire: U.S. Civil Liberties in Time of War (Boston: South End Press, 1999) 23, 30–32

92. E.B. Long and Barbara Long, The Civil War Day by Day: An Almanac 1861–1865, (Garden City, New York: Doubleday & Company, Inc., 1971) 199; Note, on April 21, 1962 certain exemp-tions were granted, 202

93. Harlan Horner, Lincoln and Greeley (Champaign, IL: Greenwood Press, 1971)

94. Roy Basler, ed., Abraham Lincoln: His Speeches and Writings, (New York: Da Capo Press, 2001)

95. Paul Rodgers, United States Constitutional Law: An Introduction, (Jefferson, North Carolina: McFarland, 2011) 109

96. William Marvel, Lincoln's Darkest Year: The War in 1862 (New York: Houghton Mifflin Harcourt, 2008)175–220; Allen C. Guelzo, Lincoln's Emancipation Proclamation: The End of American Slavery (New York: Simon and Schuster, 2006) 157–203; Bruce Carnahan, Act of Justice: Lincoln's Emancipation Proclamation and the Law of War (Louisville: University of Kentucky Press, 2007) 126–128

97. The Louisville Democrat editorial, http://opinionator.blogs.nytimes.com/2012/09/21/lincolns-great-gamble/

98. http://opinionator.blogs.nytimes.com/2012/09/21/lincolns-great-gamble/

99. David Brion Davis, The Problem of Slavery in the Age of Revolution, 1770–1823 (Oxford University Press, 1999) 213–254; Charles F. Irons, The Origins of Proslavery Christianity: White and Black Evangelicals in Colonial and Antebellum Virginia (Chapel Hill: University of North Carolina Press, 2008) 1–22; Steven Mintz and John Stauffer, The Problem of Evil: Slavery, Freedom, and the Ambiguities of American Reform (Amherst, MA: University of Massachusetts Press, 2007) 24

100. Donald M. Jacobs, Courage and Conscience: Black & White Abolitionists in Boston (Bloomington: Indiana University Press, 1993) 21–46; Joan D. Hedrick, Harriet Beecher Stowe: A Life (New York: Oxford University Press, 1995) 93–94

101. John Russell Hawkins, Centennial Encyclopedia of the African Methodist Episcopal Church, Volume 1 (Philadelphia: Book concern of the A. M. E.

Church, 1916) 8–10; Irons, 1–13

102. Albert J. Raboteau, "African-Americans, Exodus, and the American Israel" in African-American Christianity: Essays in History, edited by Paul E. Johnson (Berkeley: University of California Press, 1994) 1–9

103. Sandy Martin, "The Achievement of National Unity, 1865–Present," in The Baptist River: Essays on Many Tributaries of a Diverse Tradition, edited by William Glenn Jonas, Jr. (Macon, Georgia: Mercer University Press, 2008) 87–88; C. Eric Lincoln and Lawrence H. Mamiya, The Black Church in the African American Experience (Chapel Hill, North Carolina: Duke University Press, 1990) 1–114; Junius P. Rodriguez, Slavery in the United States: A Social, Political, and Historical Encyclopedia, Volume 2 (Santa Barbara, CA: ABC-CLIO, 2007) 99–106

104. Burrus M. Carnahan, Act of Justice: Lincoln's Emancipation Proclamation and the Law of War (Lexington: University of Kentucky Press, 2007) 126–128; Mitch Kachun, Festivals of Freedom: Meaning and Memory in African American Emancipation Celebrations, 1808–1915 (Amherst, MA: University of Massachusetts Press, 2003) 103–104

105. Gilson Willets, Inside History of the White House: The Complete History of the Domestic and Official Life in Washington of the Nation's Presidents and Their Families (New York: The Christian Herald, 1908) 208

106. Lerone Bennett, Jr., The Shaping of Black America (Chicago, IL: Johnson Publishing Co., 1975) 192–193. Unfortunately, Bennett does not credit the source.

107. Hondon B. Hargrove, Black Union Soldiers in the Civil War (Jefferson, NC: McFarland, 2003) 7–9

108. E.B. Long and Barbara Long, The Civil War Day by Day, An Almanac 1861–1865 (Garden City, New York: Doubleday & Company, Inc., 1971) 630

109. Robert V. Remini, The House: The History of the House of Representatives, (Washington, DC: Library of Congress) 186; Randall Norman Desoto, We Hold These Truths (Maitland Fla.:

Xulon Press, 2007) 140; Darlene Clark Hine, African Americans: A Concise History (Upper Saddle River, NJ, 2012) A-9

110. John Francis Ficara, Black Farmers in America (Lexington: University of Kentucky Press, 2006)

111. Jay Winik, April 1865: The Month That Saved America (New York: HarperCollins, 2002) ix–xi

112. Glenna R. Schroeder-Lein and Richard Zuczek, Andrew Johnson: A Biographical Companion (Santa Barbara, CA: ABC-CLIO, 2001) 266

113. T. Adams Upchurch, Abolition Movement (Santa Barbara, CA: ABC-CLIO, 2011) 96

114. Joseph Bliss James, The Ratification of the Fourteenth Amendment (Macon, GA: Mercer University Press, 1984) 245–246; United States Congress, House of Representatives, House Documents, Volume 85; Volume 442, 102

115. E.B. Long and Barbara Long, The Civil War Day by Day, An Almanac 1861–1865 (Garden City, New York: Doubleday & Company, Inc., 1971) 696

116. E.B. Long and Barbara Long, The Civil War Day by Day, An Almanac 1861–1865 (Garden City, New York: Doubleday & Company, Inc., 1971) 200

117. Ibid. 686

118. W.E.B. Du Bois, Black Reconstruction in America, 1860–1880 (New York: Atheneum, 1992) 188–235

119. Ibid. 474

120. Ibid. 603

121. Ray Allen Billington, Martin Ridge, Westward Expansion: A History of the American Frontier (Albuquerque: University of New Mexico Press, 2001) 349–350; Rogers M. Smith, Civic Ideals: Conflicting Visions of Citizenship in U.S. History (New Haven: Yale University Press, 1999) 304; Du Bois, 219–223;Eric Foner, Reconstruction: America's Unfinished Revolution, 1863–1877 (New York: HarperCollins, 2002) 199–203

122. Foner, 228–280

123. Foner, 346–380; Eric Foner, Freedom's Lawmakers: A Directory of Black

Officeholders During Reconstruction (Baton Rouge: Louisiana State University Press, 1996)

124. Foner, 412–601

125. Heather Cox Richardson, The Death of Reconstruction: Race, Labor, and Politics in the Post-Civil War North, 1865–1901(Cambridge, MA: Harvard University Press, 2004) 122–224; Rayford W. Logan, The Betrayal Of The Negro: From Rutherford B. Hayes To Woodrow Wilson (New York: Da Capo Press, 1997)

126. David Levering Lewis, W.E.B. Du Bois: A Biography (New York: Macmillan, 2009); Ida B. Wells and Alfreda Duster, Crusade for Justice: The Autobiography of Ida B. Wells, (Chicago, University of Chicago Press, 1991); Cornelius L. Bynum, A. Philip Randolph and the Struggle for Civil Rights (Champaign: University of Illinois Press, 2010)

127. Charles Euchner, Nobody Turn Me Around: A People's History of the 1963 March on Washington (Boston: Beacon Press, 2010); http://mlk-kpp01.stanford.edu/index.php/encyclopedia/encyclopedia/enc_march_on_washington_for_jobs_and_freedom/; Patrik Henry Bass, Like A Mighty Stream, (Philadelphia: Running Press, 2003)

128. David W. Blight, American Oracle: The Civil War in the Civil Rights Era (Harvard University Press, Cambridge MA, 2011) 236

129. John F. Kennedy Presidential Library and Museum, Boston, Massachusetts. http://www.jfklibrary.org/Asset-Viewer/9EKJbHBCs EaVSQuCd-wdigA.aspx]

130. Philip S. Foner ed., The Life and Writings of Frederick Douglass (International Publishers: NY, 1952) 246

131. Karen Price Hossell, I Have a Dream, (Chicago: Capstone Classroom, 2005) 26-28

Milestones to Remember for Sesquicentennial Celebrations

September 22, 1862 President Lincoln issued the Preliminary Emancipation Proclamation

December 31, 1862 First "watchnight"

January 1, 1863 President Lincoln signed the Emancipation Proclamation

May 22, 1863 The War Department issued General Order 143, creating the United States Colored Troops

July 1—3, 1863 Battle of Gettysburg, Pennsylvania was fought, producing the largest number of casualties in the American Civil War, and was the turning point toward Union victory

November 19, 1863 The Gettysburg Address by President Lincoln

April 8, 1864 The 13th Amendment to the Constitution, which abolished slavery in the U.S., passed the Senate.

January 31, 1865 The House of Representatives passed the 13th Amendment, completing passage by the full Congress.

February 1, 1865 President Lincoln approved the Joint Resolution of Congress submitting the proposed 13th Amendment to the state legislatures, for approval before ratification.

June 19, 1865 Freedom for the enslaved in Galveston, Texas was the final act of emancipation and origin of Juneteenth celebrations.

December 6, 1865 The necessary number of states ratified the 13th Amendment.

Credits/Sources

Pages ii and iii, Viewers of EP, photos courtesy of The Henry Ford

Pages 6-7, Library of Congress, Prints & Photographs Division, Theodor Horydczak Collection, [LC-H8-C01-062-D]

Pages 8-9, Library of Congress, Prints & Photographs Division, [LC-USZ62-41678]

Page 11, Constitution, Charters of Freedom, The National Archives

Page 12, Library of Congress, Prints & Photographs Division, [LC-USZ62-53345]

Page 13, The First African Baptist Church of Savannah. Image courtesy of Documenting the American South, The University of North Carolina at Chapel Hill Libraries

Page 14, Library of Congress, Prints & Photographs Division, [LC-USZ62-103801]

Page 15, Reverend Richard Allen, Bishop of the African Methodist Episcopal Church. Image courtesy of Documenting the American South, The University of North Carolina at Chapel Hill Libraries.

Pages 16-17, Penn School with students. From the Penn School Collection at the UNC-Chapel Hill Wilson Library. Permission granted by Penn Center, Inc., St. Helena Island, SC.

Pages 18-19, Georgia Scott

Page 20, The Weekly Contribution Box, Courtesy of Rare Books & Manuscripts Department, Boston Public Library

Page 23, Paul Cuffee

Page 24, Library of Congress, Prints & Photographs Division, [LC-USZ62-51900]

Page 25, (T) Library of Congress, Prints & Photographs Division, [LC-USZ61-1822], (B) Theodore Sedgwick Wright, African American Clergy. Image courtesy of the Randolph Linsly Simpson African-American Collection, Yale Collection of American Literature, Beinecke Rare Book and Manuscript Library

Page 26, (T) Henry Highland Garnet. Portrait by artist James U. Stead

(B) Sojourner Truth. Prints & Photographs Division, [LC-USZC4-6165]

Page 27, (T) Lydia Child. Courtesy National Portrait Gallery, Smithsonian Institution / Art Resource, NY

(B) Library of Congress, Prints & Photographs Division, [LC-USZ62-15887]

Page 28, Cover of Uncle Tom's Cabin, first edition. Courtesy of the Division of Special Collections, Archives, and Rare Books, University of Missouri at Columbia.

Page 33, (T) Library of Congress, Prints & Photographs Division, Reproduction of a painting by Charles T. Webber [LC-USZ62-28860], (C) [LC-USZ62-7816], (B) [LC-USZ62-40596]

Page 34, Library of Congress, Prints & Photographs Division, [LC-USZ62-5092 DLC]

Page 36-37, The Branded hand, © Massachusetts Historical Society, Boston, MA, USA / The Bridgeman Art Library. Used by permission.

Page 38, Library of Congress, Prints & Photographs Division, [LC-USZ62-38902]

Page 39, Negro Plot. Image courtesy of Documenting the American South, The University of North Carolina at Chapel Hill Libraries

Page 41, Library of Congress, Prints & Photographs Division, [LC-USZ62-52577]

Page 42, Library of Congress, Prints & Photographs Division, [LC-USZ62-2472]

Page 43, (T) Obsborn Perry, (B) Lewis Sheridan Leary, Courtesy Oberlin College Library Special Collections

Page 44, (T) Library of Congress, Prints & Photographs Division, [LC-USZ61-748], (B) ([LC-USZ62-7817]

Page 45, Shields Green. Image courtesy of West Virginia State Archives, Boyd B. Stutter Collection

Page 46, Library of Congress, Prints & Photographs Division, [LC-USZC4-1724]

Page 47, slaves on cotton plantation

Page 48, Library of Congress, Prints & Photographs Division, [LC-USZ62-14834]

Page 50, Library of Congress, Prints & Photographs Division, [LC-USZ62-62195]

Page 51, Library of Congress, Prints & Photographs

Division, [LC-B815-518]

Pages 52-53, The War for the Union 1862--A Bayonet Charge, from Harper's Weekly, July 12, 1862. Courtesy National Portrait Gallery, Smithsonian Institution/Art Resource, NY

Page 54, Library of Congress, Prints & Photographs Division, [LC-DIG-CWPBH-03384]

Page 55, Library of Congress, Prints & Photographs Division, [LC-DIG-CWPB-01088]

Page 57, Library of Congress, Prints & Photographs Division, [LC-DIG-CWPB-03928]

Pages 58-59, Library of Congress, Prints & Photographs Division, [LC-B817-7926

Page 60, Library of Congress, Prints & Photographs Division, [LC-DIG-PPMSCA-19305]

Page 61-67, Preliminary Emancipation Proclamation

Pages 68-69, Library of Congress, Prints & Photographs Division, [LC-USZ62-5334]

Page 71, Watchnight service at St. Peter's A.M.E. Church in St.Louis, Missouri. Photo courtesy L.D. Ingrum Gallery & Studio

Page 73, Wales Window. Photo courtesy 16th Street Baptist Church, Birmingham AL

Page 74, Harriet Jacobs. Image courtesy of Documenting the American South, The University of North Carolina at Chapel Hill Libraries

Page 75, Annie Burton. Image courtesy of Documenting the American South,

The University of North Carolina at Chapel Hill Libraries.

Pages 77-82, The Emancipation Proclamation.

Page 83, Digital Library of Georgia [SS8H6 (c)

Page 84, Hubbard Pryor, The National Archive

Pages 86-87, Library of Congress, Prints & Photographs Division, [LC-DIG-CW-PBH-03374]

Page 87, Library of Congress, Prints & Photographs Division, [LC-DIG-PPMSCA-36454]

Pages 88-89, "Juneteenth" – acrylic on canvas painting. Copyright © 2010 Synthia Saint James.www.synthia-saintjames.com

Page 90, Juneteenth Parade, Virginia Commonwealth University Library

Page 91, Juneteenth celebration at Sabayet, Inc. Photo courtesy L.D. Ingrum Gallery & Studio

Page 92, Library of Congress, Prints & Photographs Division, [LC-DIG-PGA-02595]

Page 93, Library of Congress, Prints & Photographs Division, [LC-USZ62-105555]

Page 94, Library of Congress, Prints & Photographs Division, [LC-DIG-CWPBH-00554]

Page 95, Library of Congress, Prints & Photographs Division, [LC-USZ62-2814]

Page 96, Slater, R. P. Niagara Movement founders, 1905, 1905. W. E. B. Du Bois Papers (MS 312). Courtesy Special Collections and University Archives, University Libraries, University of Massachusetts

Amherst

Page 97, Marian Anderson

Page 98, Library of Congress, Prints & Photographs Division, [PPM-SC-00048]

Page 99, Library of Congress, Prints & Photographs Division, [LC-USZ62-111167]

Page 100, Library of Congress, Prints & Photographs Division, [LC-U9-32937-32A33]

Page 101, Barack Obama.

Pages 102-103, Photo by Paul Schutzer, Time & Life Pictures/Getty Images

Page 104, President Barack Obama addresses Joint Houses of Congress

Page 104, President Barack Obama. White House Photo/ Lawrence Jackson

Page 105, President Barack Obama and Michelle Obama. Photo by Mark Ralston/AFP/Getty

Page 105, Supporters of U.S. President Barack Obama at Election Night watch party at McCormick Place November 6, 2012 in Chicago, Illinois. (Photo by Chip Somodevilla/ Getty Images)

Page 105, President Obama shares the EP with a group of African American seniors and children. Official White House Photo by Pete Souza

Page 110, Colonial flag

Page 112, Library of Congress, The second battle of Bull Run, fought Aug. 29th 1862. [LC-USZC4-1738]

Page 114, Slave advertisement

April 9, 1866 Congress passed civil rights bill—over President Andrew Johnson's veto—that bestowed citizenship to all persons born in the U.S.

July 9, 1868 The 14th Amendment to the Constitution was ratified. It granted citizenship to "all persons born or naturalized in the United States" and protected their civil rights.

February 3, 1870 The 15th Amendment was ratified by the states. It forbade any state from depriving a male citizen of his vote because of race, color, or previous condition of servitude.

100 years ago Blacks in the U.S. had scarcely celebrated 50 years post Emancipation when World War I erupted in Europe in August 1914. The 14th and 15th Amendments had not yet hit their half-century anniversaries when on April 2, 1917 the U.S. declared war against Germany. WWI centennial celebrations will begin in 2014 and the ongoing story of African American emancipation will be interwoven in those remembrances.

More than a million African Americans responded to draft calls, and about 370,000 black men were inducted into the army. Despite the recent memory of slavery and overwhelming conditions of the day, African Americans faced WWI with a sense of civic duty, as an opportunity to demonstrate patriotism, a way to earn the right to equal citizenship. Surely, if they sacrificed for the war, their country would reward them with greater civil rights.

200 years ago *Freedom's Journal* first published 1827 by African Americans in the north and then distributed covertly to Blacks throughout the country.

500 years ago on January 22, 1510, King Ferdinand of Spain authorized 50 enslaved Africans to be sent to Santo Domingo, the start of systematic transport of African slaves to the New World.

1516 Enslaved Africans aboard a Spanish caravel rebel, killed the crew, and sailed home. The first successful slave rebellion recorded in the New World.

For information about special discounts for bulk purchases, please contact

Urban Ministries, Inc.
Department #4860
P.O. Box 87618
Chicago, IL 60680-0618

cust_ord@urbanministries.com
1-800-860-8642
www.urbanministries.com

The authors are available to speak at your live event. For more information or to book an event, contact
kevmcgr@pipeline.com and vmaiathomas@hotmail.com

e-book is available from:
Amazon Kindle, Barnes and Noble Nook, Kobo, Sony, and Apple iBookstore
For bulk e-book sales contact INscribe Digital at inscribedigital.com or 415-489-7512

Scripture quotations are taken from The Holy Bible, King James Version.

Cover and interior design by Georgia Scott georgiaworldwide@gmail.com

Manufactured in the United States by STL Graphics Group, Inc.
1066 National Parkway, Schaumburg, IL 60173

First hardcover edition 2/13

1 2 3 4 5 6 7 8 9 10

ISBN 978-1-60997-876-1

ISBN 1-60997-876-5